Common Sense Investing

By:

Fred McAllen

Contents

Common Sense Investing

Introduction

The late Will Rogers said it best.

"I'm more concerned about the return OF my money than with the return ON my money". *~Will Rogers*

ABOUT THIS BOOK

This is a "tell-it-like-it-is" book. There is no fluff, no journalistic slant, just the unvarnished truth. I was a certified financial planner, stockbroker, and portfolio manager, but now I am only an individual investor just like you, and I'm tired of the Investment Firms and the Wall Street clique misleading the investing public by not giving you the full story.

I have been trading the markets for more than 20 years in stocks, bonds, mutual funds, and options. It's not difficult, but if you listen to the 'Talking Heads' on the financial news networks, stock pickers that have their own radio and TV shows, and follow their advice while blindly entering the investing world with no knowledge of your own, then you will certainly lose.

In Trading and Investing there are more theories, plans, stock pickers, investment vehicles, gimmicks, scams, and Snake Oil Salesmen than at any other time in the past.

There are crazy people on TV pushing buttons that make all sorts of goofy noises to tell you whether to buy or sell. However, the skeptics that keep up with those wonderful investment tips claim they are a miserable failure.

Some think you might as well throw darts at a financial newspaper to reveal the investment of choice.

There are others who claim a certain amount of success by giving a chimpanzee a Financial News Journal and let him 'point' at which stocks to buy.

There are companies that develop software for computers to trade for you. It's so easy! And you've seen it on TV, **so it 'must' be true!**

There are Financial Advisors that work out of the trunk of their car canvassing your neighborhood looking for anyone with a dollar to invest who will answer the door.

There are Investment Representatives working phone banks cold calling anyone brave enough to answer in search of the next sale.

No wonder so many believe they are safe to just put their money in a Mutual Fund and forget about it. At least you have an excuse when you answer the phone or the door; you can tell the salesperson, "Sorry, I already have an investment."

Problem is, having an investment and investing wisely are two totally different things. Most every investor has no idea what to invest in or why they are invested in 'It', whatever 'It' is. They rely on the advice of so-called professionals to make their investing decisions, and are constantly and consistently misled.

Throughout this book you will come to understand 'WHY' you have been misled. When a Wall Street Guru, TV host, or a Financial Advisor gives you advice, there is almost always an ulterior motive involved, money for them – not you.

Did your investments get crushed in the last stock market crash? No, not in 1929, I'm talking about 2000 to 2002, and/or 2008. Most investors got a rude awakening when they opened their year-end statements for the past 10 years, because the Bear Market of 2000 was only the second time in history that the market was down three years in a row, then right back down after the all time high in the DOW in 2007.

Are you confused by the daily gyrations of the stock market? Are you upset that you lost a bundle by listening to a salesperson hungry for a commission? Are you ready to give up on the stock market, and cash in at any price? The talking heads on the business shows continually profess a bullish stance, no matter what the market is doing. They can always put a 'positive spin' on it.

Most every one of them will profess the Buy-and-Hold Strategy for investing. But you will quickly learn why they do this, why this strategy does not work. Never has, and never will.

Ignore their opinions. That is the first rule, and don't forget it.

No one knows where the market is going tomorrow, let alone in the months and years further down the road. Just because the stock market has averaged an annual return of about 10.2% since 1926 does not mean that you can expect that rate of return to continue in the coming year, next 5 years, or even the next 10 years. Just because you may not be retiring soon does not mean that you can afford to ignore what is going on in the stock market.

If you have been investing since 1982, or perhaps since early 1995, you were probably ecstatic with your returns through the first quarter of

2000. But then the market dramatically and swiftly reversed direction, and it dropped faster than it rose. Then after decimating portfolios large and small, the market turned and moved to an all-time high in 2007 giving you hope once more, only to reverse again and drop to another low.

Did you sell at or near the top and put the proceeds into cash? You probably did not. Did you sell after your stocks or mutual funds fell 10%, then 20%, then 30%, and perhaps 90% in some cases? Probably not, since you thought the market would come back, as it always has. I will give you the statistics and facts to show you why Buying-and-Holding is not a successful strategy in the long run because the intermittent Bear Markets continually rob you of the profits... You'll be surprised by the outcome.

Let me tell you something very important. I know you have heard it, and it is true; "The market has always come back". But *this* is what you are never told: Just because the 'market' comes back, that *never* means your investments will come back, too. Some do, many do not. Historically the general market has come back, but also 'historically,' the same stocks that were once the 'Stock Market Darlings' are not usually the ones that came back with the market. Most stay down and never come back.

Perhaps you have followed the widely touted Buy-and-Hold investing approach. And if you are like most investors, you have no game plan for cutting your losses or taking your profits. I can promise you, lacking an investing strategy and blindly following the buy-and-hold approach can lead to financial ruin. It can wipe out years of investment profits in a short time, and it can take years for your portfolio to recover, if ever. Don't fall for the Buy-and-Hold *RUSE*, even though a majority of financial professionals tout it. This is the same crowd that also tells you that dollar-cost averaging is a sound investment approach. Check it out for yourself. Has your own dollar-cost averaging worked for you? Probably not.

Dollar-cost averaging is great when stock prices are rising, but can send you to the 'Poor House' when they continue to fall. One of the most critical rules of investing is *never* average down. It is a loser's game. Think about all the unfortunate and uninformed investors who still own Amazon, Dell, Cisco, EMC, AT&T, Intel, GE, Eastman Kodak, Xerox, WorldCom, Palm, and hundreds of other past high-flyers. Those investors got killed by continually buying more shares on the way down, or by holding on to their original shares bought at much higher prices.

Is There a Better Way to Invest?

Is there a smarter way to handle your investments, to protect your profits, and to steer clear of bear markets before they decimate your portfolio? Yes. The approach is called Common Sense Investing, and it works. In this book you will see compelling data on successful approaches that beat the market indexes over decades. The strategies are simple so that you can use them yourself with little work.

After reading this book you will understand both sides of the Buy-and-Hold myth and why using Common Sense and some simple strategies when investing is a more successful, sensible, risk-averse, and unemotional approach to investing in the stock market or Mutual Funds.

By presenting you with the facts and figures of many investing theories and scenarios, you will be educated on the market, the market history, the sales pitches you will likely hear, and the valuable strategies and tools to use to make your own decisions to be a successful investor.

My objective here is fourfold.

- First, I want to provide you with the rationale and facts indicating why Common Sense Investing is a superior investment strategy compared to the ever-popular buy-and-hold strategy.
- Second, I want to provide you with profitable strategies that are simple to understand and easy to implement.
- Third, I want to help you avoid future bear markets and protect your principal.
- And last, I want to help you maximize your returns, both in good times and in bad.

In writing this book, I have assumed that you have some knowledge of investing and index funds. My emphasis is on the importance of using Common Sense Investing and how to use it to improve your investment performance, while limiting your risk and protecting your principal.

Throughout this book we will focus on:

- How you, the investor can come out ahead in the stock market in the long run
- How and Why investors keep getting killed in the short run with periodic bear markets
- We will debunk the buy and hold myth
- The complete story on missing the best days *and* missing the *worst* days will be provided
- The best strategies to use when investing

You will see, in very real terms, losses suffered in bear markets often exceed the gains earned in bull markets. Bull and bear market cycles are reviewed in detail, including secular bull and bear markets where there are long periods of time when the market does nothing and you are biding your time. That is no way to make money.

Also you will be given the truth, the REAL story, about the poor record of the market experts. You will also see the advantages of Common Sense Investing using index funds, sector funds, and leveraged funds. We will cover the characteristics of exchange-traded funds and the substantial benefits they offer investors.

Most importantly, we will cover everything you wanted to know about investing using common sense but were never told by the Wall Street gurus, the financial magazine articles, or financial radio and TV shows. The critical characteristics of successful investing are provided, as well as six key points about Common Sense Investing that you need to understand. And you will learn why being 'Out of the Market' at certain times is the best strategy to protect your capital and preserve your retirement.

The 'general market knowledge' included in this book, and especially market history, is critical for your knowledge base. Learning how the market has performed in the past not only prepares you to recognize when these problems are about to occur in the future, but by the end of the book you will learn how to avoid the worst times to be invested.

It *is* about learning to use plain common sense, knowledge of the market, and implementing tactics available to you as an investor to be successful.
Let's get started.

<u>CHAPTER ONE</u>

Stocks Stink

Let's get one thing straight:

> ***I do not recommend that the average investor buy individual stocks, ever!***

I'm going to let you in on a little secret real early here, and I hope it gets your attention. Most stocks just downright stink.

And I'm not just talking about the ones you own, or the ones I own, although at times through the years I've owned plenty of terrible stocks. No, most stocks *really* do stink. Here's why.

Nearly two-thirds of stocks will underperform a diversified index. For instance, the Russell 3000 index is a stock market index of US stocks, comprised of the 3,000 largest and most liquid stocks based and traded in the U.S. Keep in mind, this index covers 98% of all 'Investable' stocks in the US.

Now, here's the deal. A research study conducted by Blackstar Funds covering stocks traded on all three major U.S. exchanges for 23 years from 1983-2006, which by the way was a very bullish time period for the stock market, found the following:

- 64% of stocks underperformed the Russell 3000 during that span, dividends included.
- 39% of stocks had a negative lifetime total return. **Two out of every five stocks lose money**.

- 19% of stocks lost at least 75% of their value. **Almost one out of five is a really bad investment**.

Did that get your attention? Then how about this:

- The mean compounded annual return of the 8,054 stocks in Blackstar's study was ***-1.06%.***

Think about that for a second. In what was considered a bullish time for stock returns, U.S. stocks on average actually *lost* money.

Nope, no silver lining in this cloud!

You're probably expecting me to say: "Just ignore all these bad statistics because You and I, we are smarter than the average bear, and we can find winning stocks. No problem!"

I really hate to burst your bubble, but only a VERY small percentage of stocks -- 14% to be exact -- delivered compound annual returns of greater than 20% during the period covered in Blackstar's study.

It doesn't take a Rocket Scientist to figure that one out. Meaning, that small 14% of 5,869 stocks was responsible for almost all of the gains of the Russell 3000 from 1983-2006.

How hard is it to find a stock that will advance 20% per year? Of the 5,869 stocks on major U.S. exchanges, only 248, or about 4% of them, had compounded annual returns of 20% or more over the 10 year period from 2000 - 2010.

Let's take a look at few of the big winners:

Stock	10-Year Annualized Return
Hansen Natural (Nasdaq: HANS)	54%
Green Mountain Coffee Roasters (Nasdaq: GMCR)	49%
Quality Systems	42%
Middleby (Nasdaq: MIDD)	34%
Goldcorp (NYSE: GG)	27%
Apple (Nasdaq: AAPL)	27%
Penn National Gaming	23%

Data from Yahoo! Finance and Capital IQ, a division of Standard & Poor's

Sure, Apple is on that list, but don't get excited yet. Apple was already a household name in 2000, but that was pre-iPod, iPad, and iPhone, and competitors like **Dell** and Gateway were eating Apple's lunch in the personal computer market at the time. If you were savvy enough to spot the 'Gold trend' before it really started to take off and ride Goldcorp to huge gains, then you are smarter than most. The other names on the list were all small companies back in 2000, and probably not on most investors' radar screens.

All of this is to say that out of a large universe of nearly 6,000 stocks, the chance of having even minimal exposure to any of these 248 big winners was slim to none, and 'Slim' has left the building, so to speak.

Let's be Realistic

History hates winners, always has. Let's go back even further. Imagine it were 1980 and I told you that in 30 years, **Eastman Kodak**, Bethlehem Steel, General Motors, Emery Air Freight, Polaroid, and **Xerox** would either be bankrupt or be trading for less than they were in 1980. What would you say? You would call me crazy, nuts, insane! Probably call the guys with the **Straitjackets** and send me to a **Rubber Room**. These were some of the leading companies of the day, the Stock Market Darlings.

Let's get even more Realistic

Look back at that table above of the 2000 - 2010 big winners. Are Apple, Goldcorp, Hansen Natural and Middleby likely to repeat their great performance of the decade? In realistic terms, let's see what they would have to do.

- Apple would need to sell somewhere in the neighborhood of ***1.2 billion*** iPhones between 2010 - 2020.
- Goldcorp's annual production would have to increase by 11 times, which is NOT going to happen, or the price of gold would need to rise to $13,100.
- Hansen Natural would need to become the household drink of choice by selling some $90 billion worth of its Monster beverages every year by 2020. That would be three times Coke's current annual sales!
- Middleby would have to sell $11.2 billion worth of commercial ovens and equipment. Now realistically, just how many restaurants are there in the U.S.?
- Green Mountain Coffee roasters would need to sell ***$65 billion*** worth of coffee machines and coffee every year by 2020, more than six times Starbucks' current annual sales!

When a little Common Sense and logic are applied, the realistic chances of a repeat performance, or even a continued performance of these winners becomes unrealistic, to say the least.

Now let's look at five of the 'Big Winners' from 1983 – 2006, **American International Group (AIG), Bear Stearns, Citigroup, Fannie Mae, and General Motors.** Since then:

- General Motors went bankrupt.
- Fannie Mae was put into receivership
- The other three each lost more than 90% of their value.

Bear Stearns was bought out by **JPMorgan** for a fraction of its previous value after being decimated by the housing and mortgage crisis, and there's still a very real chance that AIG and Citigroup face more devastating losses. As of 2010, AIG still owes the U.S. government $102 billion for its massive bailout and any cash it can possibly squeeze from asset sales and its depressed insurance operations may not be enough to cover the deficit. Citigroup has excess exposure to consumer banking that makes it extremely vulnerable to more pain in the housing market and new restrictions on consumer credit.

Big winners. Now big losers. Certainly makes you question the pure 'Buy-and-Hold' approach, doesn't it? Well, it should!

Fool's Strategy

Inherently, Investors try to find the next 'Winner.' Try to 'Pick' the next Microsoft, WalMart, or Apple. This is a 'Fool's Strategy.' Some even dabble in Penny Stocks trying to accomplish this elusive task hoping to 'Get Lucky.' That is NOT investing. That is playing the lottery.

How many of us are actually smart enough and lucky enough to find those 4% of stocks that will turn out to be big winners? As I said, "Slim and None, and Slim has left the building." In fact, you'd be very fortunate to find **just one** long-term 20% winner in your lifetime.

Stocks are simply too risky for the average investor. With the accounting scandals, SEC investigations, crooked corporate financial officers, managed earnings, and earnings targets missed by only a penny, why should you take a chance on picking the wrong stock or the right stock at the wrong time and being hit with a big loss?

It is much more prudent, and far less risky, to invest in appropriate index funds, sector funds, or exchange-traded funds.

With these funds you have a diversified portfolio and bad news from one company will not affect your investment.

For instance, investing in the S&P 500 index fund, known as 'Spider' traded on the exchange under the ticker symbol 'SPY,' you are invested in 500 of the biggest and best companies in the country, and your portfolio is not leaning toward any one sector.

Another alternative would be the 'Diamonds,' an index of the Dow Jones Industrial stocks, and 30 of the biggest companies in the world. This index trades under the ticker symbol DIA.

Or you might want to consider the Tech-heavy Nasdaq. By investing in the Qs, ticker symbol QQQQ, your investment would be in 100 of the biggest companies traded on the Nasdaq and would lean toward technology.

And if you want to invest in 'The Overall Market' then consider the iShares for the Russell 3000 index, ticker symbol IWV.

Mistakes for Investing

Has your Investment Portfolio performed as well as you expected? Has it declined in value? Do you dread opening your statement? Are you still in the 'Red'?

Throughout the past 10 years, most individuals are forced to answer those questions – No –Yes – Yes – and Yes, respectively. Many have had to postpone retirement, and in some cases lost their retirement entirely.

The vast array of investing options are seemingly mind-boggling. Most individuals do not know whether to invest in stocks, bonds, annuities, whole life policies, or mutual funds, so the easy way is to trust someone else to make the decisions and hope for the best. Unfortunately, that seldom works, at least not in the investor's favor.
There are common mistakes that most every individual makes when investing. Let's look at just a few:

1. Keeping a portfolio of individual stocks when you lack the time and expertise to monitor them. If you own just a handful of individual stocks, you're taking on two kinds of risk. One is the overall market risk (systemic risk) and the other is the risk associated with a particular stock and the underlying company.

With individual stocks, even if you have the time to monitor them, there are numerous risks involved. The company could miss expected earnings by one penny, announce a dismal outlook, be hit with a lawsuit, or any number of things can decimate the stock's price and the results can be catastrophic to your portfolio.

2. Failure to diversify. Putting all your eggs in one basket.

In case you forgot, remember the stories about Enron employees who lost it all? Some were 100% invested in the company's stock. Sure, that is the absolute worst case scenario, but look at many other companies like AOL, Yahoo, or GM. Will AOL or Yahoo ever return to their lofty values? Probably not. Never allow your portfolio to lean heavily toward a single stock or industry.

3. Owning a handful of mutual funds and thinking that you're diversified.

Review the funds' holdings. For example, if your portfolio is heavily weighted toward the health industry, then a health industry downturn could cripple you. Know what your Fund invests in.

4. Showing up late to the party.

Buying at the wrong time is a classic mistake. This inherently causes the investor to 'throw in the towel' when the market declines and take a huge loss. When the economy is good, stock prices are rising, and everything seems just peachy, many will jump on the 'band wagon' expecting to see the value of their investments increase. Problem is, the party may already be winding down. There may be little, if any, advance in the portfolio, and then the bottom falls out.

And the absolute worst mistake:

5. Failure to educate yourself.

All mistakes made in planning for retirement or investing will normally fall into this category. Most people either have no desire to learn or think they don't have the time to learn about investing. This creates a huge mistake in itself. Without basic knowledge and understanding of the market and price movements, you are relegating yourself to ONE of THREE choices.

1. **Guess and take chances.** (and you will surely lose) Guessing has never worked – you might as well be investing your hard-earned money in Lottery tickets.

2. **Do nothing.** Doing nothing is not a plan, so you can never expect to be prepared for the future.

3. **Trust someone else to decide for you.** This is sometimes more fatal than doing nothing, as you will see shortly.

Through the years I can seen numerous individuals completely rely on someone else for advice, and countless times be disappointed in the results. After taking a beating by watching the bottom line on their statements dwindle, they continue to listen to the Advisor who *SOLD* them the investment. That's the 'Fox guarding the hen house!" Many are told by their Advisor to not even open their statements and assured that holding the investment will eventually pay off.

Fire your Financial Advisor!

Yes, that is a bold statement.
But in today's world, the term 'Financial Advisor' means little or nothing. Unlike in years past when your investments were advised, made, and handled by a Stock Broker with years of experience under his belt, that is no longer the case.

The 'Modern Day Financial Advisors' are being recruited from internet job posting sites like Monster and Hot Jobs by the Investment Firms in need of sales personnel. Yes, the major Investment Firms compete for what is referred to as "Assets under Management." And in order to increase these assets, investment money must be placed with their firms. Your Money!

To accomplish this all-important goal, the Investment Firms must have sales personnel to actively sell investments to the public (you).

Here is where it gets interesting!
Investment Firms actively solicit sales people by listing job openings on Internet sites and also contacting unemployed persons who have posted a resume on the Internet.

Now, in order for these new recruits to 'Legally' sell investments, they must first be licensed. This is quickly and easily accomplished by the Investment Firm providing or purchasing a short online course for the new recruit, and then paying the fees for them to take the necessary exam. Once the recruit passes the exam, this person can now legally sell you investments.

This is insane!

In a matter of a few short weeks, an unemployed individual with absolutely no Capital Market or Investment experience whatsoever, suddenly becomes a salesperson AND '**Your Financial Advisor.'**

This person is responsible for making YOUR Investment decisions that will ultimately be your retirement!

Where is the knowledge?

Where is the experience?

Has this person ever bought or sold even 'ONE' Security?

Your Retirement depends upon this inexperienced individual?

During the past few years this practice has become the standard. New recruits are sometimes instructed to purchase one (1) share of an investment. Thus, when asked by the potential client if the investment is 'safe,' the salesperson can assure the client it is safe, because he/she owns it themselves.

Therefore, in reality what happens is the commissioned salesperson "Advises" you to invest in whatever investment product is currently paying the highest commission, or whatever the Investment Firm may currently have in their inventory that they need to "Unload."

I have seen these salespeople sell 30-year Bonds to 70-year-old widows during a bear market when interest rates were 1%, using a sales pitch that the Bond pays 2% more than the individual's CD.

This is nuts!

Think back for a moment, what were you advised to invest in when the market was at an all time high? What were you told when the value of your investment declined? Were you prepared in any way for the decline?

Were you advised to Buy-and-Hold? Many investors have never recovered from the Bear Market in 2007-08. Many have never recovered from the Bear Market in 2000-02.

Why is It?

If a Sports Guru on TV professes that a favorite team will surely lose this weekend, and not only that, have a dismal losing season, most individuals may disagree! Might even think the Guru was nuts! But if a TV personality on a financial network expounds on their beliefs about the market and the world of investing, some people swallow it 'Hook Line and Sinker.' What most do not realize is that one of the personalities on a popular financial network who consistently gives updates and opinions about the market and trading was a 'Mail Clerk' before being hired as a commentator.

Common Sense Conclusion

Not at all. There is no Common Sense in turning out classes of new recruits every week on the investing public with absolutely no Capital Market experience whatsoever. Providing these people with a pocket full of sales brochures, a laptop computer, and a list of investments that are currently paying the highest commission and expecting them to meet the Firm's pre-defined sales quotas has absolutely nothing to do with investing successfully. And unfortunately, these are only a couple of examples of the thousands I have witnessed. You are the ONLY one who has YOUR MONEY and your best interest in mind.

And listening to TV personalities should always be deemed Entertainment, NOT advice. You are nothing but 'Ratings' to them. And if they can sensationalize what is happening at that very moment to keep you watching, then they are successful, not you.

CHAPTER TWO

What is Common Sense Investing?

Common Sense Investing can be defined as making investment buy and sell decisions using both Common Sense and a mechanical trading strategy which employs one or more indicators and/or proven strategies. That sounds more complicated than it is. The objective of a mechanical trading strategy is to employ a successful system of being invested in the market during up trends and to be either out of the market in cash (or in a short position) during down trends, especially during brutal bear markets.

Common Sense Investing can be applied to all types of investments including stocks, stock and index options, mutual funds, bonds, and futures. This book focuses exclusively on using index funds, sector funds, leveraged funds, and exchange-traded funds, but it is your choice as to which investments you prefer to work with because the principles remain the same for each of them.

Common Sense Investing is aimed at taking your emotions out of the investing equation, or at least minimizing their impact because this objective is critical to your success. Investing successfully is very difficult if you become an emotional wreck experiencing heart palpitations every time your investment either falls or advances a few cents. Investor psychology has been studied for years, has never changed, and the “herd instinct” is always rampant. This urge to follow the herd plays right into your hands, because the crowd (whether individual investors or investment advisors) is characteristically wrong at *major* stock market tops and bottoms. You will see this throughout the book, this situation will always be with us, because the emotions of dealing with investing—fear and greed—will never change.

Common Sense Investing is not a perfect investing approach; there is no such thing. Common Sense Investing cannot predict precisely when the market will change direction. But we know it always does. Therefore, if you use the available tools, a reliable common sense approach, and follow its signals, then you will exit the market when it begins to turn down and you will re-enter the market when it begins to turn up, all in time to maximize your returns and protect most of your profits.

Bear Markets are a reoccurring part of the investing cycle —YOU MUST be prepared to deal with them!

Bear Markets have been around forever. Future bear markets will arrive as they have always done, just like clockwork, about every three to four years, on the average. Avoiding these slumps is the key to protecting your hard-earned capital. Unfortunately, most investors have no clue as to the market's future direction, how the stock market really works, or how to minimize their losses. Therefore, it is not surprising that individual investors suffer the consequences, and the losses, when a bear market sneaks up and mauls them.

Bear Market Statistics

From 1950 to 1999, there were over a dozen bear markets, with the average one lasting 397 days, resulting in a loss in value of 30.9% on the average. That is a major hit on your portfolio every time that happens. The emotional pain and drain is severe because Bear Markets, unlike a market crash, just continually trade lower and lower and the investor gets to experience the pain of watching their investment value decline over an extended period of time. The average recovery period to reach the previous high was approximately 622 days (1.75 years) based on the S&P 500 Index.

When the 2000-02 bear market ended on October 9, 2002 the S&P 500 Index suffered a 49.1% drop from its top on March 24, 2000 to its bottom on October 9, 2002 which lasted 941 days.

Similarly, from the market top in 2000 to the bottom on October 9, 2002, the Dow Jones Industrial Average dropped 37.8% (the actual top was January 14, 2000), and the Nasdaq Composite Index cratered a whopping 77.9%. Hope you weren't 'Holding' those stocks.

The bear market of 2007-09 started when the market fell from its all-time-high reached by the DJIA in 2007, taking with it trillions of dollars sucked from every long term, Buy-and-Hold investor's account.

There will definitely be future bear markets. Therefore, the key to investing is to preserve your capital at all costs. That means you should take prudent actions to avoid bear markets and not be invested in stocks when they occur. If you do not exit the market to protect your hard-earned money, then your profits (if there are any) and even your principal will quickly shrink. It's like a giant vacuum, and the money evaporates into thin air.

How much can you lose in the next bear market?

Well, the crash of 1929 wiped out 86% of the value of investors' portfolios, and it took investors 25.2 years to just break even. Since then, there have been 19 bear markets, with an average loss of 33%, which took an average of 3.5 years to regain those losses. Not only are bear markets deadly financially, they can and do inflict significant emotional harm as well. Not many investors can stomach the view or their statements showing declines of 30+%. But nevertheless, it happens every few years.

NOTE: When I say "it took an average of 3.5 years to regain those losses," that is a 'general term.' Meaning, the overall market regained its losses on the average of 3.5 years. This in NO WAY means the average investor ever regained their losses. You see, after a bear market, some investments will regain their losses, many do not. This applies to individual stocks, Mutual Funds, and even index funds.

Intelligent investors know that bear markets are inevitable, and therefore you should either step aside into cash or, depending on your level of risk tolerance, you should short the market using mutual funds that are specialized for investing in bear markets or exchange-traded funds.

The experts tell you that no one can 'Time the markets,' or move in and out of the market successfully with consistency. Guess what? The experts are wrong again, as you shall see. You will learn the information you need so that you don't have to guess or make an investing decision based on emotion or someone else's opinion of where the market is headed.

In late July 2002, Lawrence Kudlow, co-host of the popular *Kudlow & Cramer* show on CNBC, jokingly said that he and co-host Jim Cramer had **"called the bottom of the 2001–2002 bear market seven times, and we will eventually get it right!"**

But this is no joke. You can't afford to depend on someone else's guesses or prognostications. You need to make your own investment decisions which you can do if you stick with the time-tested indicators and strategies which you will learn about in this book.

The Stock Market = Bull Markets + Bear Markets

"The first rule is not to lose. The second rule is not to forget the first rule."

~Warren Buffett

"In the battlefield that is the stock market, there are the quick and there are the dead!...The fastest way to take a bath in the stock market is to try to prove that you are right and the market is wrong."

*~William J. O'Neil (*How to Make Money in Stocks, 2002*), p. 54*

INVESTOR PROFILES AND CONCERNS

Who are the average U.S. stock investors? Let me give you some idea as to the makeup of the average investor and it will become more clear as to the obstacles they face in trying to equal or beat the market's performance over the long term. These numbers are averages, but extremely accurate.

Ownership of Equities in America:

- 50% of all U.S. households hold Stocks and Mutual Funds.

- 95% of investors are long-term investors.
- 85% are buy-and-hold investors.
- More than 30% of investors bought stocks during 2001.
- Less than 25% sold stocks during 2001.

- 60% of those investors based their buy and sell decisions on advice of an financial advisor.
- More than 85% of investors own stock mutual funds

A more recent investor survey conducted by CNN/USA Today/Gallup Poll by telephone of 1003 adults indicated concern about the Stock Market Decline. Some of the key findings were as follows:

- 62% follow the stock market news closely.
- 66% own stock.
- 63% of stockholders feel that owning stocks is more of a gamble than a good investment.
- 63% say that "buy-and-hold" is the best strategy for them.
- 59% have lost money in the market over the past 12 months.
- 20% have sold some stock or mutual funds over the past 12 months.
- As far as the decline in the stock market is concerned, 51% perceive it as a major problem, while 29% view it as a minor problem, and 14% think it is a crisis.
- 34% feel the decline has shaken their confidence in the economy.
- 49% will cut back on their spending.
- 42% will live less comfortably than they thought they would.
- 38% will be unable to maintain their standard of living.
- 36% will now retire at a later age.

Common Sense Conclusion

No, I'm not a big fan of statistics, since statistics can be made to say about anything, and are commonly used to say whatever the 'Prophet' needs them to say. But some of these are pretty straight forward. Meaning, 62% follow the market closely while 59% have lost money in the past 12 months. We might reasonably assume these are the same people. By the end of this book, I firmly believe you will not be a member of the 59% crowd.

Most investors have never studied the history regarding the stock market. Why is that? Many will read consumer reports before even buying an appliance. Most will read warranties, reports, payment schedules, interest rates, study gas consumption and miles-per-gallon features before buying a car. But these same people will hand over their retirement to whomever 'promises' the best return on their money and never educate themselves on the market in which their money will be invested. Kinda hard to figure.

CHAPTER THREE

Stock Market Perceptions

In early 2000, investors had no idea that the next three years would be horrendous. Just look at the massive devastation inflicted on investors during the period, where over $8 trillion in market value was erased in only 32 months from peak to trough. The biggest bear since the Great Depression simply mauled investors who were blindly following the buy-and-hold mantra. Unfortunately, all of those individuals who followed the buy-and-hold strategy watched helplessly as their investments got slaughtered and their egos shattered. How could this have happened? In a word? Perception. Perception by the uninformed at its finest.

During 1999 and 2000, the stock market was the hot topic of conversation at the supermarkets, bowling alleys, bars, and hair salons all across America, as the market soared to unprecedented heights. CNBC replaced the "soaps" as the most popular daytime entertainment medium, with its streaming stock quotes, and never-ending procession of bullish market strategists, bullish financial analysts, and bullish CEOs.

Euphoria was in the air and life was great for millions of retirees, regular folk who started investing during that time, and especially day traders who were racking up huge gains. But that all came to a screeching halt when the big bear started growling in the first quarter of 2000. The bear then unceremoniously clawed the market over the next three years, to prices not seen for five years.

Are Memories really that short?

Only 5 years after the Bear Market of 2000-2002 ended, the same thing happens once again. The Dow Jones Industrial average is approaching new all-time highs. The same crowd of Talking Heads and Gurus from Wall Street are prognosticating that the DJIA will go to 20,000. Perceived expectations, and Euphoria has returned. Bullish analysts take to the air-waves encouraging the individual investor to buy, buy, buy. Using statements like "Don't let the train leave the station without you." Insinuating the market is going nowhere but 'straight up'! But the 'Bear' returns, dissipating trillions of dollars in investor capital.

Investors Are Too Emotional and Overconfident

The stock market is a very difficult place to make money. This is not a new thought. Over the past 100 years the stock market has been punctuated with sharp, uplifting bull markets, followed by swiftly plummeting bear markets. This cycle has happened in the past, and it will happen in the future. After all, the markets are driven by people. Market cycles always repeat themselves, just as history repeats itself. The economy is cyclical. That's how it functions. People are people, and where money is at stake they react emotionally, which usually results in bad decision making, and investors have a poor track record of making money in the market.

Numerous surveys have shown that investors buy and sell at the wrong time, and they usually buy and sell the wrong investments at the wrong time. Behavioral researchers have found that the incorrect decisions which investors are prone to make are the result of overconfidence in their investment knowledge, overtrading, lack of diversification, and incorrect forecasting of future events based on recent history. Perception.

Stock market success requires that investors act independently of the crowd, use common sense, while using a non-emotional, time-tested, almost mechanical investing approach. Think about it, if fear and greed are NOT eliminated from the investing equation, then the results can be catastrophic. Acting 'independent of the crowd' means viewing prognosticators and TV show hosts as entertainment. Possibly even as comedy. That is the way it is.

Robert Safian in *Money* magazine said, "All across America, millions of people are afraid to open their account statements, afraid to look at their 401(k) balances—afraid to find out what they've lost during this long bear market and where they stand today."

That's a pretty sad state of affairs. But it did not have to be that way, if investors would only have had an investment plan that forced them to take profits as stocks and the market kept going up, and they had placed stop-loss orders on their stocks to protect them as prices collapsed. But most average investors freeze, and do nothing until the market is well off its highs. Then, as the market hits subsequent lows, investors take their billions of dollars out of equity mutual funds and begin investing their money in bonds and money markets. That's like fixing an old leaky roof after it rains. Other investors are the 'throw-in-the-towel crowd' and just give up and cash in all their investments, having endured severe emotional and financial pain. These poor souls are usually responsible for what is called 'Capitulation.' Capitulation is when the market has been trading down for an extended period of time and appears to have reached a low point, then quickly takes a dive to an even lower point as investors 'throw in the towel.'

The vast majority of individuals are not very savvy investors, even though many have above-average intelligence and consider themselves above-average investors. They do not have the time, background, or expertise to assess the market at key turning points, for example, whether the bull market is beginning or ending. They have no real investing plan and have not taken the time to educate themselves on the market, its history, how it has functioned in the past, or how to recognize possible future action.

This outcome is a result of poor timing on entry and exit points and lack of a coherent, well-researched strategy. Most investors buy and sell on a whim, a 'hot stock tip,' or they take advice from a friend, or they act based on hearing an "expert" giving his opinion on the market or a particular mutual fund or stock in the media.

Every investor must have a methodology to know when to buy and when to sell. But few, if any, investors have even thought about it, let alone have a methodology in place. Unfortunately, investors as a group invest and hope for the best. This approach is no way to build a nest egg for the future, but rather a recipe for financial disaster.

You wouldn't leave your garden untended and 'hope' that it grows, since you know that weeds would grow and kill your flowers and vegetables. The same logic applies to your investments. Being proactive is better than being non-active. That is not to say that you should become a Day Trader, an active trader, or an aggressive investor. It is saying that investing is not a static endeavor. You should watch over your investments, making adjustments as necessary to weed out the dead wood, and replacing them with more fruitful pickings. You are the best gardener for your garden of investments. Don't let the experts tell you otherwise.

Remember, just because you bought stock in good companies doesn't mean that you made a good investment. Even the so-called blue chips have plummeted from their highs to much lower levels. Throughout the 2000 to 2010 decade, in the Bear Markets of 2000 to 2002 and the following Bear market of 2008 to 2009, General Electric hit $180 ($60 split adjusted) and went to $23, and then down to less than $10; AOL Time Warner Inc. hit $95 and went to $11.50; General Motors hit $85 and went to $36 and then to $0.00; AT&T Corp. hit $58 and went to $19. This type of devastation doesn't have to happen to you, if you become a smarter investor going forward. Surely, by heeding the advice of the Wall Street crowd, you can come out way ahead, right? **Wrong!** Very wrong! Keep reading.

Market Gurus and Prognosticators

"If you ask five experts where to invest, there will be six answers; the five expert opinions, plus the right one."

~*Jonathan Clements, "Need One Expert Opinion on Investing? Here's Five."* The Wall Street Journal, *January 4, 2000*

Think about all the stock market experts' market predictions you've read or heard about for the past several years. A handful of these characters have been fired, let go, replaced, or changed firms. Even well-known technicians do not have very good track records calling the market top. Let's take a look at the forecasting accuracy of the so-called prophets of Wall Street for the years 2000 through 2003.

Consider the results of these seers in predicting the market indices just one year into the future.

Business Week publishes a list of the experts' individual predictions in its year-end issue. The number of prognosticators tracked by the magazine for the years 2000 through 2003 has varied between 38 and 65, with 50 being the average. This list represents a solid cross-section of the well-known market strategists. Some of the well-known names on a number of the yearly lists included Joseph V. Battipaglia, Elaine

Garzarelli, Edward Yardeni, Bernie Schaeffer, Edward Kerschner, Lazlo Birinyi, Jr., Hugh Johnson, Philip J. Orlando, and Jeffrey Applegate.

Table 1-1 shows the composite results of all of their forecasts over four years for the Dow Jones Industrial Average (DJIA), the Standard & Poor's 500 (S&P 500), and the Nasdaq Composite Index. The table delineates for each year the high, low, and consensus forecast of all the forecasters for each of the three popular market averages.

TABLE 1-1

Business Week Fearless Forecasts 2000 - 2003

Year	DJIA Forecast	DJIA Close	Percent Diff.	S&P 500 Forecast	S&P 500 Close	Percent Diff.	Nasdaq Comp. Forecast	Nasdaq Comp. Close	Percent Diff.
2000	14000 H			1750 H			5000 H		
	8800 L			1000 L			2000 L		
	12154 C	10768	−12.6%	1556 C	1320	−17.9%	3805 C	2471	−54.0%
2001	13050 H			1650 H			4300 H		
	8000 L			1000 L			1800 L		
	12015 C	10022	−19.9%	1559 C	1148	−35.8%	3583 C	1950	−83.7%
2002	13250 H			1535 H			2626 H		
	7200 L			920 L			1500 L		
	11090 C	8342	−32.9%	1292 C	880	−46.8%	2236 C	1336	−67.4%
2003	11400 H			1250 H			2500 H		
	7600 L			800 L			1065 L		
	9871 C	TBD		1049 C	TBD		1703 C	TBD	

As you can see, starting with the first forecast for the 2000 stock market made at the end of 1999, the forecasters had a poor record. In fact, in each of those three years their forecasts actually got progressively worse. Forecasters, as a group, were simply overly optimistic and are historically wrong most of the time.

There are always a few bears around, but even the bears didn't predict the actual lows of the market in 2002. The most inaccurate predictions were for the Nasdaq, as the actual close compared to the consensus forecast was off by 54% in 2000, 84% in 2001, and 67% in 2002. In conclusion, the "best and the brightest" appeared to be not so bright after all. To be fair, their actual stock picks for their clients could have been quite different, and perhaps closer to the mark. For the sake of their clients, I hope this is so.

STOCK RETURNS VARY BY DECADE

This subject is very important for you to know and remember. The reason is, you cannot base your investment decisions on what the market has done over the past 75 years. The convenient phrase, "The market has always come back," is so misleading. You DO NOT have 75 years to wait on your investment to materialize into the profit column.

Stock market returns are not consistent; in fact, they vary all over the map. That fact is what drives investors crazy. They never seem to know if they should be buying or selling. Listening to the advice and predictions of the Wall Street crowd further confuses the issue and many try to follow the crowd. If investors are fully invested during up trends, they can experience excellent returns. Unfortunately, the down trends can take away a good portion of their gains, if they just follow the buy-and-hold approach. Consider the wide variance in average annual stock market returns during the seven decades since the 1930s.

The 1950s, the 1980s, and the 1990s produced above-average returns in the neighborhood of 18%, while on the flip side the 1930s, 1960s, and 1970s provided less-than-stellar returns, around 6% or less. The 1940s provided a return close to the 10.2% annual return of stocks between 1926 and 2002.

One point to recognize here is the time variance. If you were invested in the 1950s or 1980s, you did OK. But what about the 1960s and 1970s? There were 20 years of investing with only an average of 6% returns. When you factor in the 'Risk' of being IN the market during those times then the picture becomes much clearer.

TABLE 1-2

S&P 500 Decade Performance Statistics

Decade	Average Annual Return*
1930s	−0.05 percent
1940s	9.17
1950s	19.35
1960s	7.81
1970s	5.86
1980s	17.55
1990s	18.21
Other periods:	
1995–1999	28.45
2000–2002	−14.59

Meaning, is a 6% return really worth being 100% at risk?

Remember that as we proceed.

As you can see, the 1995–1999 period was an anomaly, which produced abnormally high returns for those who stayed fully invested during that time period. Since the beginning of 1995, had those same investors been holding their stocks and mutual funds through October 9, 2002, they would have sustained substantial losses, depending upon their investment portfolio mix. (Remember, at that time, many investors had high exposure to the technology sector.)

Stock Returns from 2000 through 2002

The performance of the three major averages in that three-year bear market was very poor. Table 1-3 shows the widespread devastation from the highs to the lows.

Three-Year 2000–2002 Bear Market Performance

Index	High	Date	Low	Date	Percent Change
Nasdaq Comp.	5048.62	03/10/2000	1114.11	10/9/2002	−77.9
S&P 500	1527.46	03/24/2000	776.76	10/9/2002	−49.1
DJIA	11722.98	01/14/2000	7286.27	10/9/2002	−37.8

For just the year 2000, the Nasdaq Composite Index was down 32%, the S&P 500 was down 23%, and the DJIA fell 17%.

As you can clearly see, to be fully invested in stocks or stock mutual funds during a severe bear market is a frightening experience and one that should be avoided. Based on what you hear from the so-called experts, there is no way to know when a bear market is coming, or its duration. They keep professing that buy-and-hold is the way to go because in the long run you'll do fine. This ridiculous and costly advice will be tackled head-on as we proceed.

Stock Market Confuses Most Investors Most of the Time.

The stock market simply confuses most investors most of the time, always has, and it will continue to do so in the future. That is because the markets are driven by **Investor psychology and perception of events.**

For instance, when good news comes out about a stock, sometimes its price rises, and sometimes its price falls. When the Federal Reserve FOMC (Federal Open Market Committee) cuts interest rates, as it has on over a dozen occasions in the past few years, sometimes the market rises and closes up for the day, and sometimes it falls and closes down for the day. In that respect the market is unpredictable and that confuses investors, as well as the so-called professionals, although they may not admit it.

The market is continually discounting all known information and is always looking ahead, not behind. So news, whether good or bad, will impact the market in the short run. But in the long run, growth in corporate earnings and dividends, coupled with a sound economy with low interest rates and low inflation, is what will drive stock prices higher.

And when least expected by the vast majority of investors and professionals, the market will turn around and make a new bull run, with deceiving dips along the way to shake out the weak hands. And market bottoms usually occur when investor pessimism is high, the news is all bad, and no one wants to own stocks anymore.

Perception is what drives markets, not reality.

Therefore, the market races ahead while investors are hoarding their cash. The market declines while investors are hoping for a turn-around. The market moves sideways sometimes for no apparent reason. It is unpredictable. But what you will learn is to stack the odds in your favor.

First we must look at the past to understand where we have come from in order to have a better understanding of the future.

Common Sense Conclusion

Yes, the investing public has a very short memory. Studying the events and stories told of the Stock Market Crash of 1929, the same euphoria was present in 1999 and 2000. The attitudes and stories were identical, only the names changed. When the market started faltering in 2007 with the mortgage crisis surfacing, the same types of events were happening similar to 2000 and even similar to 1929. Commentators and prognosticators were professing that the DJIA would continue to advance and were completely resolute in their claims while assuring the listeners how stable the economy was. The stock market highs with the backdrop of banking and housing issues sounded much like a story published in the London Times regarding the 1929 crash that read:

> "The Roaring Twenties, the decade that led up to the Crash, was a time of wealth and excess. Despite caution of the dangers of speculation, many believed that the market could sustain high price levels. Shortly before the crash, economist Irving Fisher famously proclaimed, **"Stock prices have reached what looks like a permanently high plateau."**"

Whether it's 1929, 1999, or 2007, you hear the same bullish crowd professing their beliefs and their misguided attempts at predicting the future.

Common Sense tells us to never rely on a salesperson, TV personality, or prognosticator to make our investing decisions. Their interests and yours are not the same. When you are advised to buy-and-hold, remember what history tells you.

> **"Anyone who bought stocks in mid-1929 and held onto them saw most of his or her adult life pass by before getting back to even."**
>
> ~Richard M. Salsman

This also applies to current time periods, not just 1929. Many investors holding stocks purchased from the late 90s through 2000 or mid-2007 will likely not live long enough to get back to even. Many lost it all and no longer even have the chance to get back to even.

CHAPTER FOUR

Bull and Bear Markets

Background information on Bull and Bear markets is vitally important to you, as an investor. You must have a clear picture as to how a market can trade sideways for many years, and then finally break out to new highs, but then return to the lows. Without knowing where the market has come from and how it got here, you can never be fully prepared for the future.

Looking back, individuals participated in a great bull run, if they were fully invested since 1982 or since the end of 1990, or even since the beginning of 1995. From October 11, 1990, until January 14, 2000, the DJIA rose a cumulative 396%. From 1995 through 1999, the S&P 500 Index rose at a 28% annual compounded rate. In 1999 alone, the Nasdaq Composite Index jumped an astonishing 85.6%. That was its largest yearly increase since the index was created in 1971.

Investors should have been extremely cautious in 2000, after such a huge unprecedented run-up, but they were net buyers of stock rather than net sellers right at the market top because of the unabashed euphoria and the bullish "gurus." This run-up in price like the Nasdaq experienced is what is called a "Blow-Off Top" or "Spike." It happens in individual stocks and in overall markets as well. (This type of market action is covered in my book, **'Charting and Technical Analysis.'**)

Unfortunately, bear markets arrive every three to five years (four years on average), and they can demolish your capital. It can then take years to get back to breakeven, assuming you have the stomach to hold at the bottom. Don't forget that a 50% loss in a stock or mutual fund(s) requires a 100% gain just to break even. And in the case of a 75% loss, a 300% gain is needed to break even. To recover from this magnitude of loss takes years, if ever.

Most studies have shown that investors buy at market tops and sell at the bottom—just the opposite of what they should be doing. Since investing is ruled by emotions, this situation will always occur. Fear and greed are factors that are at play when humans and their money are involved, and this fact will never change.

Stock Market Performance over 102 Years

How has the stock market performed over the last 102 years? To gain a perspective on the magnitude of bull and bear markets, look at Tables 1-4 and 1-5. This data presents all the bull and bear markets in the twentieth century, using the DJIA as the benchmark.

NOTE: Neither the Standard & Poor's 500 Nor the Nasdaq Composite Index has historical data that far back in time. Therefore, the DJIA was used to gather this data.

A Bear Market or Bull Market is defined as a decline or rise of 20%, respectively, in a major market index (such as the DJIA, the S&P 500, or the Nasdaq Composite Index). Table 1-4 adheres to this classification, but Table 1-5 has six time frames in which the change in percentage was less than 20%.

As Table 1-4 indicates, there have been 27 bull markets from 1900 through 2000, with an average gain of 91.5% and an average duration of 28.8 months (2.4 years). The average gain is skewed by the super-bullish May 1926–March 1937 time frame, in which the cumulative return was over 459%, and the November 1990 through July 1998 time frame, where the return was 300%. These outsized positive returns actually pumped up the average return during a bull market run to 91.5%.

Be aware of this fact when comparing bull markets to each other. Remember, you don't have 100 years to wait on your investment.

TABLE 1-4

Over a Century of Bull Markets

Dow Jones Industrials

START		END		LENGTH*	START	END	%CHANGE
SEPT	1900	JUNE	1901	10	54	78	44%
NOV	1903	FEB	1906	27	44	100	127%
NOV	1907	DEC	1909	26	54	100	85%
SEPT	1911	OCT	1912	14	73	94	22%
DEC	1914	NOV	1916	24	54	110	104%
DEC	1917	NOV	1919	24	68	115	69%
AUG	1921	MAR	1923	20	65	105	62%
JUN	1924	FEB	1926	21	90	170	89%
MAY	1926	SEP	1929	41	150	390	160%
JUL	1932	FEB	1934	20	40	110	175%
SEPT	1934	MAR	1937	31	85	190	124%
MAR	1938	SEPT	1939	19	100	160	60%
APR	1942	JUNE	1946	50	95	210	121%
JUN	1949	JAN	1953	43	180	295	64%
SEPT	1953	APR	1956	32	270	510	89%
OCT	1957	JAN	1960	27	410	690	68%
OCT	1960	NOV	1961	14	580	720	24%
JUN	1962	FEB	1966	45	540	1000	85%
OCT	1966	DEC	1968	27	750	975	30%
MAY	1970	JAN	1973	32	550	1050	91%
DEC	1974	SEP	1976	22	570	1025	80%
MAR	1980	APR	1981	13	750	1020	36%
AUG	1982	JAN	1984	18	790	1300	65%
JULY	1984	AUG	1987	37	1100	2750	150%
OCT	1987	AUG	1990	33	1620	3025	87%
NOV	1990	JUL	1998	92	2350	9367	300%
SEP	1998	JAN	2000	16	7400	11750	59%
OCT	2002	?	?	?	7286	?	?

27 Bull Markets
Average Length 28.8
Average Gain 91.5%

* in months

Looking at the bear market scenario in Table 1-5 we find that there have been 28 bear markets, with an average drop of –30%. The largest drop ever was the –90% tumble from September 1929 to July 1932. The next worst was the January 1973 through December 1974 period (and February 1906 through November 1907), with a drop of –46%.

Let's put it in perspective.

TABLE 1-6

Over a Century of Bear Markets

Dow Jones Industrials

START		END		LENGTH*	START	END	%CHANGE
DEC	1899	SEP	1900	10	75	54	−28%
JUN	1901	NOV	1903	30	78	44	−44%
FEB	1906	NOV	1907	22	100	54	−46%
DEC	1909	SEP	1911	22	100	73	−27%
OCT	1912	JUL	1914	22	94	72	−23%
NOV	1916	DEC	1917	14	110	68	−38%
NOV	1919	AUG	1921	22	94	72	−23%
MAR	1923	JUN	1924	16	105	90	−14%
FEB	1926	MAY	1926	4	170	150	−12%
SEP	1929	JUL	1932	35	390	40	−90%
FEB	1934	SEP	1934	8	110	85	−23%
MAR	1937	MAR	1938	13	190	100	−47%
SEP	1939	APR	1942	31	160	95	−41%
JUN	1946	JUN	1949	37	210	180	−14%
JAN	1953	SEP	1953	9	295	270	−8%
APR	1956	OCT	1957	19	510	410	−20%
JAN	1960	OCT	1960	10	690	580	−16%
NOV	1961	JUN	1962	7	720	540	−25%
FEB	1966	OCT	1966	9	1000	750	−25%
DEC	1968	MAY	1970	18	975	550	−44%
JAN	1973	DEC	1974	24	1050	570	−46%
SEP	1976	MAR	1980	42	1025	750	−27%
APR	1981	AUG	1982	16	1020	790	−23%
JAN	1984	JUL	1984	7	1300	1100	−15%
AUG	1987	OCT	1987	2	2750	1620	−41%
AUG	1990	NOV	1990	4	3025	2350	−22%
JUL	1998	SEP	1998	2	9367	7400	−21%
JAN	2000	OCT	2002	30	11723	7286	−38%

28 Bear Markets
Average Length 17.0
Average Gain −30.0%

* in months

Sometimes when looking at the 'Numbers' such as the tables shown above, it is easy to forget how the numbers are generated. For instance: The Bull Market that started in July 1932 and ended in February 1934 produced 175% gain. Yes this gain is correct, however, please note that the Bull Market started with the DJI at '40'. After reaching 390 during the previous Bull Market.

The following chart helps to put it in proper perspective.

As you can see, even with 175% gain during the Bull Market of 1932 - 1937, Investors did not recover losses from the previous Bear Market. In fact, it took more than 25 years to recover their losses. More is explained regarding this in the section on Secular Bull and Bear Markets.

During the Bear market of 2007-2009, by March 9, 2009, the DJIA had dropped -54% to 6469 (before beginning to recover) from its peak of 14164 on October 9, 2007, a span of 17 months.

The previous bear market, ending on October 9, 2002, produced a drop of –38% for the DJIA. But the S&P 500 Index fell –49% during this timeframe and the Nasdaq Composite got clobbered, dropping –78%.

The average bear market has lasted 17.3 months. But there have been some catastrophic ones, including the 35-month bear market from September 1929 to July 1932, the 37-month bear market from June 1946 to June 1949, the 42-month bear market from September 1976 to March 1980, and of course the 32-month bear market from January 2000 through October 2002.

Bear markets drops are much faster than bull market rises. For example, from January 1, 1991, to March 31, 2000, a period of 9.25 years, the S&P 500 rose from 330.22 to 1498.50 points, or a total gain of 1168.28 points resulting in a gain of 353%. In stark contrast from the end of June through the end of July 2002, the S&P 500 fell 266 points, or a loss of approximately 23% of that entire gain over a period of just two months. That's volatility in a bear market! The third quarter of 2002 produced the worst quarterly results in 15 years, with the major averages down 18% or more.

Bear Market Recoveries

Table 1-6 provides data on how long it takes to break even, assuming a buy-and-hold approach with the S&P 500 Index, once a bear market has reached bottom. Also shown is the combined time of the drop and the time to recovery.

TABLE 1-6

Time to Recoup S&P 500 Bear Market Losses

Year Began	Percent Loss	Duration Years	Recovery Time Years	Combined Time Years
1929	−86	2.75	25.2	27.95
1939	−34	1.7	2.3	4.0
1937	−55	1.0	8.8	9.8
1938	−48	3.4	6.4	9.8
1946	−28	1.8	4.1	5.9
1956	−22	1.2	2.1	3.3
1961	−28	0.5	1.7	2.2
1966	−22	0.7	1.3	2.0
1968	−36	1.5	3.3	4.8
1973	−48	1.75	7.5	9.25
1980	−27	1.75	1.9	3.25
1987	−34	0.33	1.9	2.23
1990	−20	0.25	0.6	0.85

Unbelievably, it took over 25 years for buy-and-hold investors to break even from the ravages of the Great Depression. Do you really want to wait this long just to get your money back, assuming you didn't sell at the bottom? Do you think the average investor was able to take the pain of an 86% drop and wait 25 years? I certainly don't.

From 1956 through July 2002, the average bear market lasted 421 days (1.15 years), resulting in an average loss of 30.2%. The average recovery period to reach the previous high was about 639 days (1.75 years). Excluding the 2000 bear market, the average bear market lasted 364 days and lost 29.6%.

Note that it took more time to recover from every bear market there has ever been than the duration of the actual bear market itself.

The bear market of 2000-2002 was the third longest in duration since the Great Depression and the worst since 1938. Investors should realize that these long bear markets will occur again in the future, so a strategy to protect principal must be in place in advance to avoid both the devastating loss of principal and the years of no realized gains necessary to recover to the break-even point.

Percentage Gain After Bear Market

The percentage gain after bear markets can be substantial, as Table 1-7 illustrates.

TABLE 1-7

Recoveries After Bear Markets
Percent Gain from S&P 500 Low

Bear Market Ended	2 mos. After	6 mos. After	9 mos. After	12 mos. After
June '49	13	23	26	42
October '57	1	10	19	31
June '62	14	21	27	33
October '66	12	22	25	33
May '70	12	23	40	44
October '74	8	31	52	38
August '82	31	44	60	58
December '87	13	19	18	21
October '90	11	28	28	29
October '02	15	11	29	
Average	13	23	32	37

Common Sense Investing can provide the tools you need to capture a fair percentage of these gains, as you shall see.

CHAPTER FIVE

Secular Bull and Bear Markets

You never hear much about bear markets during the optimism of bull markets, like the 1995-2000, or the 2003-2007 bull market. But it is pretty much agreed that when the market topped out in March 2000 it was either the end, or darn close to the end of the long 1982-2000 Secular Bull Market.

As Warren Buffett said, and others predicted at the time,

> **"The next 17 years will be quite different from the last 17 years."**
>
> ~Warren Buffett

And for the 2000-2010 decade, it was certainly different. There were two cyclical bull markets and two cyclical bear markets. At the end of the decade, the S&P 500 still needed to gain 36% just to get back to breakeven with its level of 2000, and the Nasdaq needed a 119% gain to get back to its level of 10 years earlier.

The last 110 years were clearly divided into three secular bull markets and three secular bear markets.

The following chart gives a clear view of how the market actually moves in the larger scale over long periods of time.

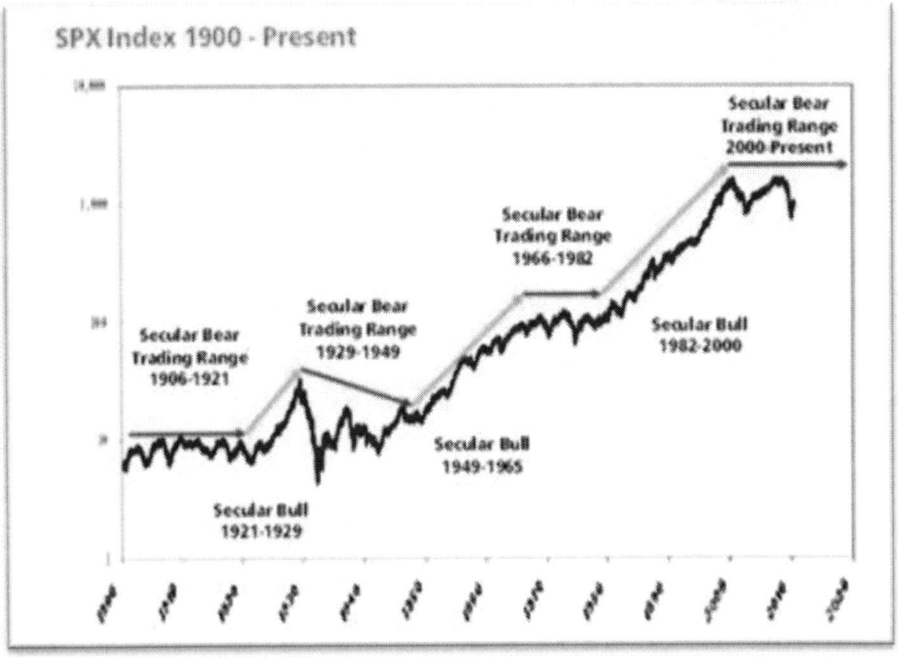

In secular bull markets, the periodic *cyclical* bear markets can be devastating, like the 1987 crash. But they are only temporary and the bull market resumes to ever higher highs.

In secular bear markets, the periodic *cyclical* bull markets can be exciting and profitable, like the 2003-2007 bull market. But they are only temporary and the secular bear just growls and takes over again.

The three secular bear markets of the last 110 years lasted for 20 years, 20 years, and 16 years respectively, which is undoubtedly where Warren Buffett came up with the “next 17 years” in 2000.

What causes a ‘Secular Bear Market?’

The simple answer is ‘Bubble Bursting.’

As the economy runs in its cycles, normal bull and bear markets occur. As the economy expands, the Bulls take over, and as the economy contracts, the Bears return. As mentioned earlier, about every 3 to 4 years, the Bulls and Bears switch sides as to who has the upper hand.

But a Secular Bull or Bear Market is different. When a 'Bubble' bursts, it takes a longer period of time to *unwind* the effects that the bubble created. For instance, in 2000 when the dot com bubble burst, the market went into bear stages. But a simple decline in prices was not enough to purge the bubble effects from the economic system.

Some believe the Secular Bull didn't die in 2000, but lived until 2007 because the U.S. government decided to inflate the real estate bubble to compensate for the pain in the economy which was caused by the bursting of the dot com bubble. Therefore, some are of the opinion that easy credit extended the life of that Secular Bull to 2007.

Regardless, after the bursting of a bubble, it takes time for the system to be purged of excesses, and during that time of purging the market will rally and falter several times. This causes the sideways trading with no real gain or at times negative investment returns for extended periods of time.

So yes, bull and bear markets occur not only over short timeframes but also over long timeframes. There were two long-term (secular) bull and two long-term bear markets for the 71-year period from 1929-1999. For the entire 71-year timeframe, the S&P 500 Index had an average annual return of 10.6%. But it was not all smooth sailing over that period. The secular bull markets from 1942 to 1965 and 1982 to 1999 produced average annual gains of 15.7% and 18.5%, respectively. But the two secular bear markets from 1929 to 1941 and 1966 to 1981 produced much lower annual average returns of –2.4% and 6%, respectively.

Let's look at just the Secular Bull and Bear markets since 1929.

TABLE 1-8

Secular Bull and Bear Markets
Stock market returns (in percent)

	1929-1999	1929-1941	1942-1965	1966-1981	1982-1999
Type of Market	Total Period	Secular Bear	Secular Bull	Secular Bear	Secular Bull
Length in Years	71 yrs	13 yrs	24 yrs	16 yrs	18 yrs
Annualized Return of S&P500	10.6	−2.4	15.7	6	18.5
Inflation Index (CPI)	3.3	−0.8	3.1	7	3.3
S&P500 Real Return	7.1	−1.6	12.2	−0.9	14.7

The above table is very important to every investor. As you can see, there can be long periods of time when the market is flat or down. **This is what most investors are not aware of.** Most individuals only hear part of the story, "The market has produced returns averaging 10% per year for 71 years." That is true when viewing only the 71-year time frame. But that is *not* the whole story, and is misleading when presented *only* in that way. The rest of the story goes like this: During that 71-year period, the Secular Bear Markets actually produced minimal or negative returns for long periods of time.

Let's look at these individually.

The following chart shows the first Secular Bear Market from 1929 to 1941. And according to the table above, that Secular Bear Market lasted 13 years and ended in 1941.

But take a close look when 'theoretically' the Secular Bear Market ended and the new Secular Bull Market began.

The new Secular Bull Market started in 1941, but the market was still below the high reached in 1937, and remained below that high until 1946. This provides the rest of the story. In theory, the Secular Bear Market ended in 1941, but in reality, the investors were still in the hole and in a trading range of the bear market for 4 more years. Therefore, the Secular Bear Market caused investors to not recognize any real gains for 17 years instead of 13 years as the table above indicates, and even longer for those who purchased near the market top prior to the beginning of the Bear Market in 1929.

PLEASE NOTE: These charts are history, but they are very important as you will see in later charts showing more current trading activity. History *does* repeat itself.

The following shows the next 24-year Secular Bull Market from 1942 to 1965, as indicated in the above table. But let's take a closer look.

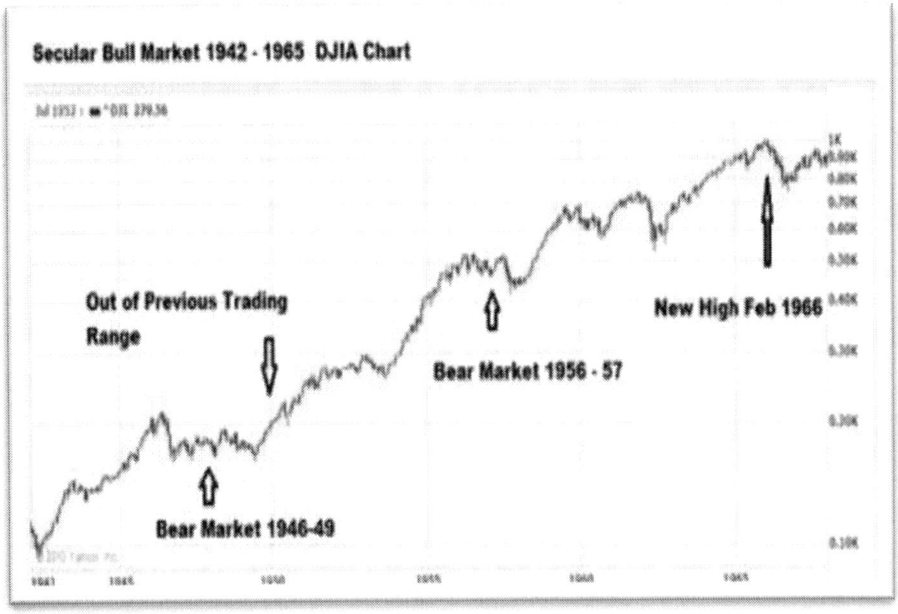

The Market had been in the previous trading range since the lows in 1932, and finally moved higher in 1949-50. This is when the investors started realizing gains from investments made in the late 20s. Some waited more than 25 years to break even.

Once again, even though the new bull market started in 1942 and in theory lasted 24 years, in reality, the Market did not trade above the previous trading range until 1949-1950, and did not move above the October 1929 highs until November 1954, 25 years later.

The point is, the time during the Secular Bull Market that investors realized actual gains was not 24 years. In reality, the gains started in

1954 and ended in 1966, or 12 years. Also, during that time of 'Overall' gains, there were 5 cyclical Bear Markets.

Even in secular bull markets there are cyclical bear markets, where prices rally and falter, rally and falter, but overall, no progress or negative progress is made. This is depicted in the above chart showing the periods from June 1946 to June 1949, 37 months, 14% decline, with no advance and again in 1953, 1956, 1960, and 1961.

The next chart shows the Secular Bear Market from 1966 to 1981 which followed the previous Secular Bull market.

Also notice the two major drops in the market in 1971 and 1975. There are numerous opportunities to make money, assuming you have the ability and willingness to follow the markets, have an investing plan, and use an approach that works.

The following chart is the Secular Bull Market beginning in 1982 and ending in 2000.

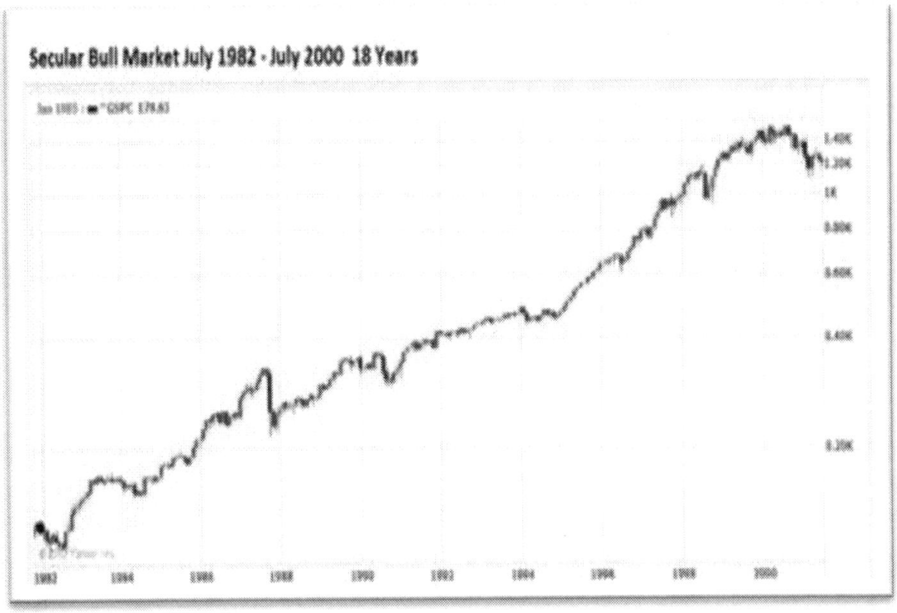

There is quite a difference in the charts of Secular Bull and Secular Bear Markets showing the market action during those extended time periods. The Secular Bear time periods are sideways while the Secular Bull time periods are advancing.

That is why it is important to have a viable investing approach. Buying and holding in a secular bear market is not a money-making approach.

And inflation always eats away at whatever returns you are able to obtain.

After inflation, the two previous secular bear markets had negative returns.

Let's now look at a 15-year chart of the S&P 500 from 1995 to 2010.

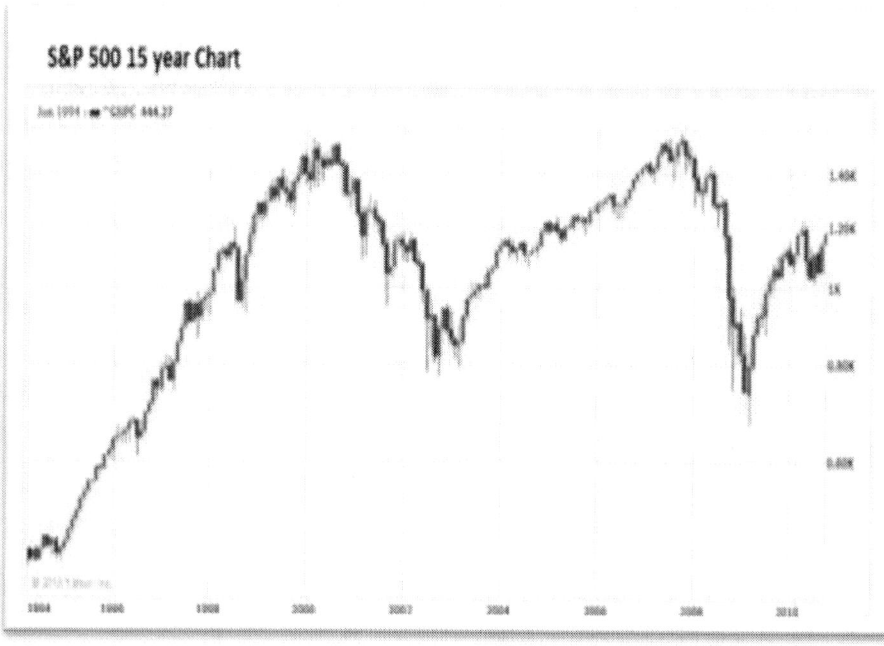

When looking at the above chart, you see the market from a distance, the big picture, so to speak. You can see that the advance starting in 1982, and depicted on the chart from 1994, ended with the high in 2000. But then for 10 years the market traded sideways. A higher high in 2007, but then a lower low in 2009 compared to the low in 2003.

The following chart is a comparison of the previous Secular Bear Market from 1966 to 1981 and the 15-year chart from 1994 to 2010.

An investor who is a chartist could have a 'Heyday' with these similarities. Realizing that history does repeat itself and market action and pricing will always show up in the charts, the comparisons certainly could create several discussions.
Please note the similarities.

Remember, history repeats itself. The bear market lows in 1971 and 1975 are strikingly similar to the lows of 2003 and 2008. Both time periods reveal a higher high between the bear markets before experiencing the lower lows during the second bear market.

Interestingly, the following chart shows the Trading Range the market continued in after the second high reached in 1972.

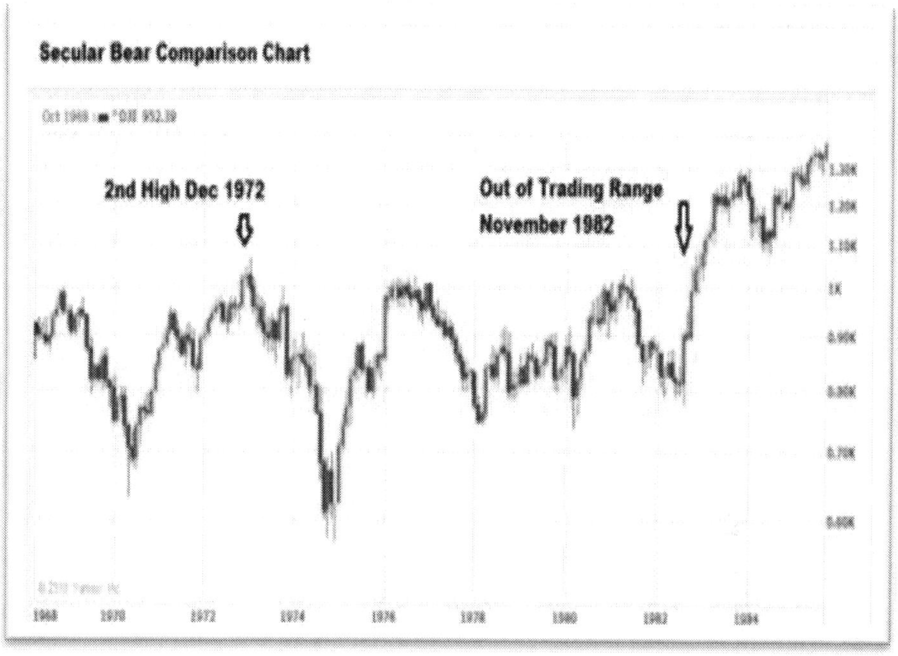

Yes, after the second high reached in 1972 that is strikingly similar to the high of 2007, the market traded sideways for 10 years before breaking out of the Secular Bear Market in 1982.

Does this mean that history will repeat itself and the market will continue in a trading range until 2017 or possibly longer? No one knows. All we can do is be prepared in the event that happens.

Now let's look at a comparison of the Secular Bull Markets from 1942 to 1965, and 1982 to 2000. Notice the similarities in the consistent advances in the market.

The question is always 'when' we will enter another secular bear market that could last 12 to 17 years or more. No one knows the answer. But simply realizing that Secular Bear Markets have always followed Secular

Bull Markets, we can only guess when the last Secular Bull Market ended.

Look at the following chart showing the Secular Bull Market beginning in 1982.

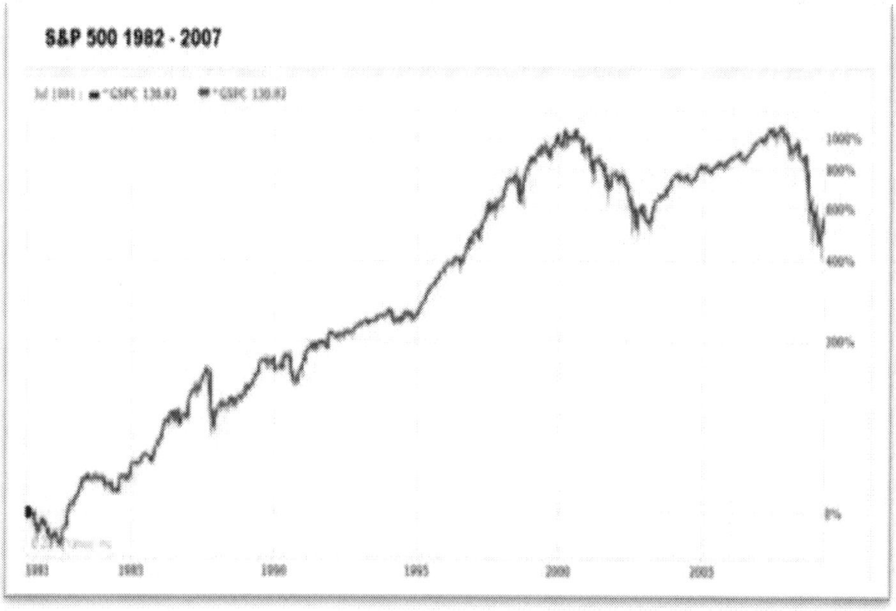

This gets extremely interesting.

Some would surmise that the last Secular Bull Market ended when the market topped out in July 2000. However, others would argue that the last Secular Bull Market did not end until 2007, which is based on the fact that the market made a higher high in 2007.

When comparing the above historical charts that are so similar, one would tend to believe that a Secular Bear Market started in 2000, or maybe it did not start till 2007.

Since we do know that Secular Bear Markets have always followed Secular Bull Markets, one must question how long the 2010 market will continue in its trading range. Theoretically, it will end by 2020. But no one knows for certain.

That is why it is absolutely imperative to have a plan for investing. You can never afford to be caught in a long period of time with no gains and possibly devastating losses. For instance, if a Secular Bear Market began in 2007, and as history has taught us, could result in a sideways market for 12 to 17 years or more, that could be devastating for investors who are expecting to have positive gains on their investments. It could also cause necessary but unexpected changes in many retirement plans.

Remember:
Since World War II, the market has seen an 18-year rally, followed by an 18-year flat period, followed by another 18-year rally—the one ending in 2000 or possibly not until 2007. That means 2010 could be just a few years into the next 18-year flat spell.

I discussed the time periods of the Secular Bear Markets and the actual time an investor was realizing positive gains was in fact less than the full time period of the Bull Market. Here is a summation of what the above charts were showing.

Here are three very important bits of investing history that every investor should memorize.

An analysis of the DJIA for 108 years from 1885 through 1993:

1. **Bear Markets consumed 32% of the time of your investment**
2. **Getting back to breakeven took another 44% of the time**

3. **Only 24% of the time was spent in net Bull Market territory.**

Common Sense Conclusion

The stock market is not a place for the individuals who think that they can sit back and rake in the profits, year after year with little risk. As you just saw, Secular Bull Markets are followed by Secular Bear Markets and vice versa. The stock market is a very risky place, where investors need to be on their toes or their feet will get burned, and sometimes burned beyond recognition. Long-term financial success in the stock market is difficult to attain, if not impossible, unless investors use a solid investing plan, develop strict entry and exit strategies, and have the psychological makeup to make tough decisions when conditions look the bleakest or the best.

As you learned in this chapter, bear markets occur often, take considerable time to come back to breakeven, and can result in significant financial loss and emotional distress. That is why investing in individual stocks or even stock mutual funds at the wrong time can be deadly to your wealth.

Recouping losses to get back to breakeven can take many years. Years that most investors do not have.

> **"It wasn't greed that killed America's retirement savings dream. It was an irrational belief in passive, buy-and-hold investment strategies."**
>
> *~William E. Donoghue*

CHAPTER SIX

Bear Market Losses

Are Real – They are NOT an illusion

If you were an investor in your twenties or thirties in 2000, then you may have time to recover from the two previous bear markets. But investors in their fifties may never recover the losses they suffered in the 2000–2002 or the 2007-2009 bear markets. Consider the following statistics from AARP:

- Many investors, and especially those over age 55, who have less time to recoup their stock market losses than those in their twenties, were devastated by the bear market of 2000. More than $7 trillion (that is equal to $25,000 for every man, woman, and child in America) went down the investment drain during that three years.
- $700 billion in retirement savings were decimated.
- A dollar invested in a Standard & Poor's 500 Stock Index Fund in March 2000 was worth about 55 cents as of August 2002.

VERY IMPORTANT:
Proponents of the Buy-and-Hold Theory will argue that the market always comes back. Historically that has been the case. But that is only half of the truth. The overall Market came back after the

dredging of 2000- 2002 to a new all-time high 5 years later, but the same individual stocks didn't come back, and seldom ever do. Yes, the DJIA reached a new all-time high in 2007, but the Nasdaq never came back to its high of 5034 that it reached in 2000. It only managed to reach 2500 before the next bear market began. The point is – Historically 'NEW' leaders always emerge to charge ahead and lead the overall Market back from bear stages. But investors have no way of knowing which stocks or funds will be the 'new' leaders, so the individual investor may never see a time when they break even.

Therefore, the Buy-and-Hold Theory only works for ***specific*** stocks at ***specific*** times.

Forget About Dollar Cost Averaging

Don't add to your investments in a bear market.

Dollar-cost averaging is another popular investing strategy bandied about in the canyons of Wall Street. It is normally used in one of two ways.

1. Some investment firms sell new investors on the idea of purchasing shares of a fund on a monthly basis. A few dollars out of every paycheck for the purchase of shares of the fund. This method is purported as being efficient for the young investor and their investment portfolio is built over time on an 'average cost' basis.

2. Another use of this strategy is to 'Add to' your investment as it drops in value. Buying more shares each time the price drops, thus reducing your overall 'cost basis' as the value of the shares decline.

Never ever, let me repeat that, ***NEVER EVER*** use dollar-cost averaging in a *bear* market. It puts you on the wrong side of the trade and the wrong side of the market when the market is tanking. Experienced traders are right when they say ***"never average down."*** Take the advice of Richard Russell (*Dow Theory Letters*, 1984):

> **"Averaging down in a bear market is tantamount to taking a seat on the down escalator at Macy's."** (Imagine the pain at the bottom.)

Imagine buying Corning at $113 (split adjusted) on September 1, 2000, and buying more shares each month as it tanked, just so that you could lower your cost basis. Corning hit a low of $1.10 on October 8, 2002. Or buying GM near its high of $80 and adding to your shares as it declined, eventually dropping to $0.00 and bankruptcy. How in the world can you ever recoup that kind of a loss?

Dollar-cost averaging in a bear market is a strategy for dummies, not for intelligent investors. That goes for stocks as well as mutual funds. There is no guarantee that your stocks and mutual funds will return to their March 2000 highs or the highs in 2007 any time soon, and throwing good money into a declining fund makes no sense at all. Remember that hundreds of funds go out of existence or are merged into other funds simply because of their poor investment performance.

MOST INVESTORS ARE NOT FACING REALITY

Most investors follow the bad advice of financial advisors. Investors are told, and believe:

- Buying a diversified basket of stocks and holding them for the long run is the best way to invest.
- Buy-and-hold is the only way to invest.
- Dollar-cost averaging is a good strategy.
- Financial advisors, brokers, and so-called 'stock market gurus' should be consulted or followed to obtain the best possible investment results. (That might be the worst strategy of all.)
- Tax consequences should always be considered in making investment decisions. (This is true. But – when the market drops from thirty to fifty percent, taxes are the least of your worries.

Believe it or not, all of these beliefs are FALSE! Many intelligent individuals are not intelligent investors. In making their investment decisions, too many investors rely only on fundamental research and totally ignore the technical indicators of stock market investing. Investors must understand that their thinking may not be realistic or accurate, and that they cannot be successful as investors by viewing the world through "rose-colored glasses."

It doesn't matter how long you peruse the quarterly financials of a company or how convinced you become the company will make a killing. If the market as a whole is headed down, your favorite company will go down with the market 9 times out of 10. Remember: **"All ships rise and fall with the tide."**

Neither should you let tax consequences interfere with sensible stock market strategies. Otherwise you will end up paralyzed and confused, and you will never sell your losers or your winners. Of course you can use effective buying and selling strategies without concern in tax deferred retirement accounts because there are no tax consequences in such accounts. But, don't assume that taking profits in regular accounts will work against you. It may or may not. Your primary concern should always focus on protecting and preserving your capital, and tax considerations are secondary to your financial well being where the stock market is concerned.

Look at it this way, would you rather 'Have' your money and pay taxes, or 'Not Have' it? Any taxes normally seem insignificant when compared to losing 30%, 50%, or more of your capital.

One of the major premises in this book is that buy-and-hold is, in fact, a loser's strategy.

That's right, a loser's strategy. You won't see that statement very often in the financial news. An entire chapter of this book is devoted to debunking the buy-and-hold crowd. Another critical premise of this book is that the safest way to invest in the stock market is to be "out" of the market in a cash account (or to be short the market), during declining periods, and to be "in" the market only during the most favorable time periods. This completely contradicts what some experts will tell you.

You will hear, **"It's time in the market that counts, not timing the market."** I will show you that the opposite is true.

INVESTORS NEED AN ACTION PLAN

Unfortunately, some investment firms do not provide fair and balanced information on investing. For example, I've come across some incomplete information in literature from Northwestern Mutual Financial Network, Edward Jones, Merrill Lynch, Morgan Stanley, U.S. Global Investors, Invesco Funds Group, Inc., and Fidelity, to name a few.

All these firms have a chart or table depicting the reduced annual returns if an investor had missed the 10 best days in the market compared to buying and holding.

They conveniently forgot to provide a chart or table showing the improved performance by missing the 10 WORST days.

In the latter case, the returns would be much higher if you had been out of the market. So, you are only getting half the story because these firms have a motive for wanting you to stay invested at all times.

- First, it reduces their overhead expenses and costs of administering the fund to have you stay put.
- Second, it eliminates any liquidity problems for the fund that could be caused by a large number of fund holders liquidating at the same time. If this happens, it could force the fund to sustain unwanted market losses from selling off holdings in order to meet the redemption needs of exiting fund holders. (Note: By charter, mutual funds are always invested, never sitting on the sidelines during a downturn.)

Your financial advisor or planner, if you have one, can help you with estate planning, retirement planning, asset allocation, insurance needs, and so on. In fact, almost 75% of investors use advisors to provide guidance. But very few, if any, financial planners have any strategy whatsoever for market declines; instead, they will advise you on investing in a diversified group of stocks or mutual funds and then leave you hanging in the breeze. They also hope you *don't* call when your statement arrives showing a decline. Diversifying is fine advice, as far it goes. But in a bear market, the stock components will drop in value. Mutual Fund values will drop. So it is entirely up to you to protect your own portfolio.

During the New York Money Show on October 23, 2002, opening day, nine investment experts made introductory presentations about their market viewpoints and what they planned to cover in their sessions over the next few days. Guess what? The experts were almost evenly split between bulls and bears. So, bottom line as an investor relying on these "experts," you were left in a quandary as to whether you should be buying or selling. I consider such conferences as sideshows for the uninformed.

Point is, you can consult 10 different advisors. All 10 of them will likely give you different advice, and all 10 will have some theory or documentation to support their beliefs. Which one is correct? Maybe none. You have to make your own investment decisions to protect your money. No one else will do it for you.

To make money and be successful in the stock market, every investor needs a plan of action based on a solid strategy that works in bull markets and especially in bear markets. Everyone is a genius in bull markets. When all stocks are rising, picking one that is advancing in not difficult. But bear markets are different. They all go down. The chance of picking a stock that is advancing in a bear market is like finding a needle in a haystack.

This is a daunting task for any investor, since many studies have shown that the majority of investors neither equal nor beat the market averages. This happens because investors have no plan, act emotionally, and they swing between the fear of a market downfall and the greed for making the most money during a market upswing. Eventually they get caught and buy at the top and sell at the bottom because they invest with their stomachs instead of with their brains.

Investing in mutual funds is really no different. DALBAR, Inc. (a leading financial-services research firm), studied the performance of mutual fund investors from January 1984 through December 2000. They found that in the year 2000 the average equity fund investor held her or his mutual funds for 2.6 years and realized an annualized return of only 5.32%, compared to a return 16.29% for the S&P 500 Index during the 17-year period studied.

Common Sense Conclusion

So how should investors participate in the roller-coaster stock market without getting heart palpitations, without losing all their profits, or worse, their initial capital, and without getting physically or mentally sickened by their losses?

It's simple really, have a plan.

A financial advisor has only one thing in mind, sell! The investment firms did not make their money through stupidity. They do not pay advisors to simply advise clients. Every advisor must meet sales quotas or face termination of their employment. The investment firms offer trips, vacations, and bonuses as incentives for their sales personnel to reach their selling goals, not investment return goals.

But you know what? There are never any such incentives offered or given for preserving and protecting the balance in your account from declines. They have no strategy for you to sell your investments at market tops, prior to market corrections, or at the beginning of bear markets. Their only strategy is for you to buy. Therefore, you will consistently be expected to purchase an investment that not only pays a commission up front at the time of sale, but will also pay trailing commissions. This provides the salesperson with continual income on your money, as long as you *hold* this investment.

You can do better, I promise.

But first, let's get Buy-and-Hold out of the way. Read on ...

CHAPTER SEVEN

Understanding Buy-and-Hold

I have previously referred to the buy-and-hold concept, or theory, of investing numerous times. But in order for you to see all sides of investing theories and have the complete truth, you need to understand everything about each theory.

Buy-and-hold is simply defined as buying a diversified portfolio of high-quality stocks, and/or a diversified group of mutual funds, and holding them for the long term—typically defined as 10 to 20 years or longer. This investing approach is well entrenched in books on investing, in mutual fund marketing literature, and in the 'double-speak' of financial advisors, academicians, and financial journalists. And as you know, it is almost impossible to change the conventional wisdom. But also remember, they do have ulterior motives.

I suspect this approach has not worked for you. For many, it never lives up to the expectations investors have for their portfolio.

According to the Chicago research firm Ibbotson Associates, based on the S&P 500 Index, from 1926 to 2001, there was a 29% probability that an investor would lose money in the market if he were investing for a one-year time frame. However, if he were to invest for a five-year period, the probability of loss dropped to 10%. For a 10-year period it dropped to 3%, and for a 15-year period there would be no loss whatsoever.

Translating these three numbers into actual dollar amounts:

A $1000 investment in stocks over the 76-year period would have been worth $2,279,000, while a bond investment would have been worth $51,000, and T-bills would have been worth $17,000. Remember now, these results apply only if you held for **76 years**!

Moreover, if the investor restricted his investments to large-cap stocks for this 76-year period, then he would have realized a compounded annual return of 10.7%, as compared to 5.3% for U.S. Treasury bonds, and 3.8% for T-bills.

Thus, the argument for buy-and-hold is that a long-term investor makes out well, while those in the market for short periods of time have a higher probability of loss.

That is true, in theory. But bear markets can significantly reduce an investor's capital. Another thing to remember is that very few investors are able to hold their investments for long periods of time such as 15 or 20 years or possibly longer. Meaning, few of us have the option of investing and never needing any of that investment for an emergency, children's education, or for some other reason. With that in mind, what will the market and your investment actually be doing at the time you need it? Will the market be in bear stages, your investment down in value?

Therefore, investors need a plan of action to limit those situations and preserve their capital.

From the market peak in January 2000 to its low on October 9, 2002, the mighty bear market cost investors a whopping $8 trillion in loss of value. If you were a part of the 'crowd,' then you stayed fully invested as you were taught to do by the proponents of the buy-and-hold philosophy, and you suffered your share of those devastating losses. Unfortunately, many investors still hold their demolished portfolios and are hoping to recoup their losses. But from the size of their losses, it seems doubtful they will ever see their money again. Many of the stocks that were purchased for $50 a share and upwards are now selling for under $10 a share and may never return anywhere close to their highs.

You would think while investors were getting pummeled during that bear market that they would have the common sense and the fortitude to cut loose from buy-and-hold and bail out. But that is not what a CNN/USA Today/Gallup Poll found in a random poll of 720 investors taken on July 29-31, 2002 (when the market had already dropped by a substantial percentage for the year).

Overall, according to the survey, 63% of the respondents felt that buy-and-hold was the best strategy for them, 30% felt some other strategy which they did not name was better, and 7% had no opinion.

Buy-and-hold is not a myth.

But the **'fallacy'** is that the buy-and-hold strategy can be successfully applied to all of the stocks in your portfolio because, in practice, **it only works with selective stocks**.

All investors should diversify to insulate themselves from the risk of any particular stock totally 'going south.' So, if you own a portfolio of say, ten stocks, the odds that the buy-and-hold strategy will produce positive results for all of your holdings over a period of time is most likely nil. Even a few bad apples with large losses can reduce your overall return to less than you could have earned in an index fund.

So this is where the market makers get you. There are plenty of stocks in the universe for which buy-and-hold has worked well, or might work well, but that is the **short list** and those stocks are in the minority. An advisor may cite an example of one of these stocks which has the effect of keeping you in the game, all the while you are sustaining significant losses on the majority of your holdings. The myth is that if you hold on long enough despite the pain you will ultimately recoup the losses you sustained on the whole shebang. **Don't bank on it, because it rarely happens.**

Buy-and-Hold Arguments: Pro's and Con's

Most of the Wall Street professionals, including newsletter writers and money managers, speak convincingly about the wisdom of the buy-and-hold strategy. There are numerous arguments put forth by high-level Wall Street professionals and mutual fund executives as to why buy-and-hold is a superior strategy.

Problem is, they have an ulterior motive for doing this. And at the same time, most of their arguments lack sufficient detail or facts to back up their claims. They may refer to one or two academic studies published in financial journals a few years ago to back themselves up.

But by reading those studies you will find that the key assumptions made by the authors are not always clearly spelled out. There seems to always be something missing (like avoiding the 10 worst days in the market), and this leaves the investor with a problem as to the study's methodology, timeframe, choice of investment vehicle, and hypothesis being tested.

I want you to see every side of the equation so you can decide for yourself. So, let's take some of the more popular buy-and-hold arguments, and then present the flip side to that argument.

The Argument:

No one can predict what the market will do in the future. Therefore, it is best to buy-and-hold good-quality stocks and a bevy of diversified mutual funds because good companies will always persevere in the long run.

The Counter argument:

It is true that no one can predict the market's future course. That does not mean that you just give up and keep your money invested *100%* of the time, when you know with *100%* certainty that bear markets will occur and take away a major percentage or all of your profits every three or four years. Buy-and-hold is a defeatist attitude that only costs you money and grief. There is no reason to default into this defective strategy when a better one is available. It is true that a diversified portfolio will cushion the blow in bear markets, but in bear markets you will still have losses in the portion invested in equities.

Buy-and-hold has had disastrous returns, even for the well-known "nifty-fifty" stocks of the 1970s. If you remember in the 1970s the vogue was to invest in the 50 largest blue chip growth companies with the expectation that they would continue to provide investors with substantial returns on their investments. Those who invested in Xerox under that theory saw their investment lose 72% of its market value in the 1973–1974 bear market; and it took them 24 years to recover their money. From October 1990 until May 1999, Xerox rose 1100%, but then dropped 93% from May 1999 through December 2000. So an investor buying $100 worth of Xerox stock in October 1990 saw the value of his stock rise to $1,200 by May 1999, and then saw it plummet by $1,116 in value ending up with a loss of $16 over the 10-year period! Polaroid Corporation lost 90% of its value from its peak price, and took 28 years to break even again, and then went into bankruptcy. Avon Products stock was stagnant for 24 years, and Black & Decker took 23 years to get back to its peak price. More currently, Enron peaked at $90 in August 2000 and then traded at $0.38 by year-end 2002, and you know what happened to it. And hundreds of Internet stocks and technology stocks lost 90% or more of their value in just three years. Even the stable stocks and growth stocks suffered substantial damage; witness what happened in the banking sector, Internet sector, automobile sector, and chemicals.

To look at the double speak of the Mutual Fund managers you only need to know that equity mutual fund portfolio turnover was around 15% in the 1950s through 1964, rose to 48% in the early 1970s, to 75% in 1983, 111% in 1987, dropped back to 74% in 1993–1994, and rose again to 90% in 2000 and 111% in June 2002. Clearly, mutual fund managers do not practice buy-and-hold with the funds entrusted to them, but somehow find it appropriate for the individual investments of their clients. I have already stated the reason for this which is that mutual funds cannot stay in business if the fund holders embark on large-scale redemptions from their funds.

By implementing specific investing strategies, an investor can successfully invest in the market and avoid the major portion of downtrends while being fully invested during the major portion of up-trends.

The Argument:

If you were out of the market and missed the 10 or 20 best trading days, then your average annual return would be much lower than if you had been in the market and fully invested on those days under the buy-and-hold approach. Therefore, you must be in the market all the time so you don't miss the best time periods.

The Counter Argument:

The argument that you would have had much lower annual returns if you missed the best 10 days, 20 days, 30 days, or whatever trading days of the year is true. But keep in mind that the 10 best days are not consecutive, but occur periodically throughout the year. Second, the purveyors of that information rarely tell you the other side of the story: that you would have had an even higher annual return if you had missed the 10, 20, or 30 WORST days. And missing the 10 worst days produces a far better overall return for you than not missing the 10 best days. For the actual statistics, see the section later titled "Missing the Best and Worst Days (Months) in the Market."

The Argument:

There are no investing strategies that work as consistently or as well as buy-and-hold over long periods of time.

The Counter Argument:

Of course there are strategies that beat buy-and-hold over the long run. But they are not discussed very much in print or on the airwaves because of the vested interest in favor of buy-and-hold. There are many strategies that have outperformed buy-and-hold, and there are many more in print that do so by wide margins. The ones that I've chosen to present in this book have the advantage of being easy to put in practice, and they are simple strategies that have shown consistent performance over many years. (Discussion of specific strategies begins in Chapter Eight.)

The Argument:

The famed Peter Lynch, money manager in the 'hey days' of the Fidelity Magellan Fund said, "There are no market- timers in the Forbes 400."

The Counter Argument:

True, there probably are no timers on the Forbes 400 list. But except in some few instances, those people didn't make their vast fortunes through the stock market. They made it by founding businesses that grew into stellar companies. They have great wealth because they are the major shareholders in their own companies: Malcolm Forbes in Forbes, Bill Gates in Microsoft, and John Templeton in Templeton Funds. These people have to buy and hold or they lose their grip on the companies they own and control.

It is interesting to note that when Peter Lynch was running Magellan Fund, his portfolio turnover in some of his best-performing years approached 300%—certainly not a buy-and-hold practitioner.

In sum, Common Sense Investing is not a perfect system for making money, nor is it guaranteed. But over a 10- or 20-year period, Common Sense Investing can produce significant returns exceeding buy-and-hold with less risk. And if an investor uses leverage, the results can be outstanding, as you will see later.

The Argument:

People who need to rely on their savings and need access to that money in the near future such as those nearing retirement age or those needing to finance their children's college education should be mostly out of stocks to ensure that their funds will be there when they need them.

The Counter Argument:

Advising investors who will need access to their money in the near term to exit stocks entirely is questionable advice. To the contrary, the market is the only place to grow your funds and to keep up with inflation. Today, people are living longer, which means they run the risk of consuming their money if it isn't working at maximum capacity, which means they must keep open the opportunity to achieve capital appreciation from their stock and mutual fund investments. You only want to be out of the market when a bear market begins or is in progress.

The Argument:

According to many academicians, stock prices are a "random walk," and future stock price movements cannot be predicted. They also argue the efficient-market hypothesis, which holds that all the information about a stock is baked into its stock price instantly. In this scenario, no one can consistently beat the market over the long term because the stock price has already taken variables into account.

The Counter Argument:

Yes, you hear the academicians profess the random-walk theory and the "efficient-market hypothesis" to bolster their case that no one can consistently out-perform the market. First, if those two hypotheses were true, then only the lucky few investors would ever make any money in the market. Clearly, there are individuals and firms who do beat the buy-and-hold strategy, and with less risk. Secondly, even during this information age we live in, where all the news about a company is instantaneous, that never prevents a company stock price from suffering in a bear market.

More Nails in the Coffin

You won't see "The Buy-and-Hold **Myth**" mentioned very often on financial shows or written about in the financial press. That is because the buy-and-hold mantra has been pummeled into investors' psyches by the top Wall Street professionals for decades. If the stock market rose 80% of the time, with corrections of 5 to 10% along the way, then perhaps the buy-and-hold strategy would make sense. But I will let the record speak for itself as you shall see later on.

Many individuals believe that time is on their side and no matter what happens in the short run, that they will come out of it okay in the long run. But you must remember, what you do in the short run is very important to your long-term performance. During 2002, there were numerous stories of individual investors whose portfolios dropped by 50% or more, and they had to go back to work or postpone their retirements. The same was true in 2008. Many investors sat idly by watching as their portfolios were decimated to the tune of 35, 45, 60%, or more.

Common Sense Conclusion

Remember this:

The closer an investor is to retirement or needing his capital, the more dangerous a buy-and-hold strategy becomes.

It's simple, really. Your financial advisor gets paid whether your Investment account increases in value or not. It's called, *FEES*. Every Fund has them, and these fees are deducted from your account even if your account balance declines with the market.

An extended period of sideways or flat market with no advance can kill the account of a Buy and Hold Investor. The Secular Bear markets prevent any return, especially when you are paying continual fees to a Fund while the account value is declining. The only thing a crystal ball tells us is "throughout 100 years of trading there have always been Bear Markets", and all we can do is prepare for them.

CHAPTER SEVEN

Diversification

Sure, diversification through allocation of investments in a portfolio with say 60% stocks, and 40% bonds, can help reduce market risk. Overall you have less risk than the investor who is 100% fully invested in stocks. This is what many financial planners will tell you. Of course the more your portfolio is 'watered down', obviously the less risk you have and the less opportunity you have for gain.

But the optimum scenario is to be 100% in stocks in bull markets to capture the highest returns for your portfolio. And to be 100% in cash or cash equivalents (or to be short the market) during bear markets.

By watering down your portfolio with bonds, you are denying yourself the incremental profits from stocks. Since bear markets are inevitable, then prepare by selling your stocks and mutual funds before the bear takes hold. Common Sense Investing can help you achieve that goal and keep you on the right side of the market.

I want to emphasize here that this book and Common Sense Investing are not about stock selection. The key to Common Sense Investing is knowing when to enter the market and when to exit. That applies to Stocks, Mutual Funds, Index Funds, and even Bonds. I'm just talking about the 'Market'. All stocks are bad unless they go up in price, and even the best stocks lose money in bear markets. At least 80% of stocks decline in a bear market. And as you likely know, IF stocks decline, so does your Mutual Fund, retirement account, etc..

The art of the game is to be in the market at the right times, and to be out of the market at the right times. Picking the right stock or Fund is only secondary to this overriding principle, because a rising tide will lift all stocks and a falling tide will lower all stocks regardless of the stock you may happen to own at the time.

What leads to people's downfall in following an investing plan is, like most other things with the stock market, - "Execution."

When it is time to exit, many will rationalize that this time will be different. Or, this year the decline in the market will not happen because of certain factors, etc. Therefore, they stay put despite the historical record and the readings of the indicators. Or, you may say that even if the market should fall, the story behind the stock is so compelling that it cannot possibly decline. This is a gambler's approach, not an investor's approach. The odds are heavily against you and you are bucking the odds. You are betting 'Against the House' and the 'House' always wins. It is far better to forego the profits you *hope for* or anticipate from that stock than for it to disappoint you and fall under the weight of the bear market. Preservation of capital is the ultimate consideration, and well worth the cost of foregone profits.

Diversifying will not save your capital.

Look at Table 2-1, which provides a comparison of specific percentage allocations of stocks and bonds with their resultant risk and returns. Being 100% invested over the 76-year period from 1926 through 2002, each rolling 12-month period produced an average return of 13% with a risk of 22% (risk is the variability in return over the 76-year 12-month rolling periods. In this example with a return of 13%, the risk of 22% means that the return fluctuates between a high of 35% to a low of 9%.).

TABLE 2-1

Percentage Mix of Stocks and Bonds
12-month rolling periods:
January 1926–September 2002

Stocks/Bond Ratio	Return	Risk
100% stocks	13%	22%
90% /10%	12.20%	20%
80%/20%	11.50%	18%
70%/30%	10.90%	16%
60%/40%	10%	14%
50%/50%	9.20%	12.50%
40%/60%	8.50%	11%
30%/70%	7.90%	10%
20%/80%	7%	9.10%
10%/90%	6.50%	8.70%
100% bonds	5.80%	9%

A 60–40% split between stocks and bonds reduced the return to 10% from 13%, with risk falling from 22% to 14%.

Take NOTE: The 'Risk' is still greater than the 'Return' in every scenario.

And at the other extreme, if you were all in bonds, your appreciation suffered greatly with a 5.8% return, and a 9% risk factor.

As expected, the higher the return, the higher the risk. What if I told you that you could obtain the returns of buy-and-hold (being 100% invested), but with half the risk. It is really simple.

All you would have to do is to use the "best six months" strategy, as explained later.

You will see that you can beat buy-and-hold and be out of the market for six months in a money market account. That means that you are getting a better risk-adjusted return for your money. The sweetener is that you are accruing interest in a money market account while almost everyone else's portfolio is sinking in value. More on the later, but first, let's look at risk, a very important factor in investing.

Recognizing Risk

Investors usually do not consider the risk of investing until they've lost a big chunk of their money. And most believe that by diversifying, they eliminate risk. This is so *NOT TRUE*.

Unfortunately, most investors are fixated on how much money they are going to make in the market, not on "how do I protect my capital from eroding." What many do not understand is that all investments are risky. The alternative is to invest in the U.S. Treasury bill, which is the safest investment there is, but the return on investment (the yield) is pitiful compared to stocks or equity mutual funds over long time frames.

Usually the more risky the investment, the greater the return. That is why Junk Bonds pay very high return. There is more risk. However, in a down market, the added risk results in worse-than-average returns.

Every investor has to decide, before investing in any investment vehicle, what level of risk he or she is comfortable with. For example, can you withstand a drop of 20% in your portfolio in a 4-week or a 52-week time frame without feeling upset and concerned? If this level of risk is unacceptable, then the investor should consider a diversified equity portfolio of index funds composed of growth and value, domestic and international, small cap and large cap. Diversification is necessary to limit the downside risk. To further reduce risk, a certain percentage of bond index funds should be included, since bond funds typically rise when stock funds decline, so there is a counterbalance. But remember, in diversifying to this extent, your return will be 'watered down' and you will probably be disappointed in the results.

Common Sense Investing can be successfully used with a diversified index fund portfolio to lower the risk of buy-and-hold even further. So on a risk-adjusted basis, Common Sense Investing used with a diversified portfolio should be able to equal or beat buy-and-hold without a problem.

Buy-and-Hold Is Risky

Investors must understand that buy-and-hold is a very risky strategy compared to Common Sense Investing. Buy-and-hold exposes investors to every twist and turn in the market, and big drops in the market can devastate the value of their portfolios. Common Sense Investing may underperform buy-and-hold in bull markets but should outperform it in bear markets. Investors who dismiss Common Sense Investing as a viable investing strategy are therefore doing themselves a major disservice.

This last bear market is just one example of many over the last 100 years, where buying and holding stocks or stock mutual funds was not a wise, rational, or a money-protecting strategy. Actually, it was financial suicide.

Don't forget that there is something called the "opportunity cost" of money. It relates to the income foregone because an opportunity to earn income was not pursued. If you are not earning interest or capital gains on your money, then you are losing out. If you were 100% invested in stocks from 1999 to 2002, or from 2007 to 2009 and you lost 50% of your money, then you sure got whacked.

Had you sold in early 2000 or in 2007 instead of staying fully invested, and put your money into a money fund earning an average of 2% per year until after the Bear Market, you would have been way ahead.

By being fully invested during the bear market(s):

- You gave up the opportunity to earn an average of 2% a year. So in this case you lost 50% of your money when you could have earned 6% (2% over three years, not including compounding), so your opportunity cost was 56%.

- The additional opportunity that is lost is when you are fully invested, you are unable to take advantage of buying 'In' at the lowest point in the market and reaping the rewards of the gains when the market recovers. Imagine if you had sold out, went to cash or Money market in 2000 or in 2007 and waited for the 'Opportunity' to re-enter the market. Buying in at, or near the lowest point. Yet, if you are fully invested during the bear market, then you are only hoping to 'Recover' your losses during the next upswing. Big difference, huh?

Given the choice, I would much rather be counting my gains than hoping just to get back to 'Even.'

Missing the Best and Worst

DAYS (MONTHS) IN THE MARKET

Numerous articles refer to the meager investment performance realized by the hypothetical investor who was unlucky enough to miss the best days or months in the stock market. The argument goes like this:

"Unless you are invested all the time using a buy-and-hold approach, you have no way of knowing when the market's best days or months will occur. Since these big up moves do not occur that often, an investor must be fully invested to take advantage of them."

Unfortunately, this scenario is only half the story.

The other half of the story should be told. And that is the very positive impact of missing the *WORST* **days or months in the market.**

Research on Missing the Best and Worst Time Periods

In 1994, Towneley Capital Management, Inc., commissioned a study conducted by Professor H. Nejat Seyhun, Ph.D, at the University of Michigan School of Business Administration to research the effect of daily and monthly market swings on a portfolio's performance, for two time periods: 1926–1993 and 1963–1993. The study analyzed the best and worst days' and months' performance.

The title of his research document was "Stock Market Extremes and Portfolio Performance." A few of the critical findings of the study were as follows:

- From 1926 through 1993, a capitalization-weighted index of U.S. stocks (NYSE) for the entire period, ASE (American Stock Exchange) from July 1962, and Nasdaq from December 1972 gained an average of 12.02% annually (buy-and-hold). An initial investment of $1.00 in 1926 would have earned a cumulative $637.30.

- From 1926 through 1993, missing the 48 BEST months, or only 5.9% of all months, decreased the annual return to 2.86% from 12.02%, and the cumulative gain amounted to only $1.60.

- From 1926 through 1993, eliminating the 48 WORST months, or only 5.9% of all months, increased the annual return to 23.0% and the cumulative gain swelled to a total to $270,592.80.

- From 1963 through 1993, missing the best 1.2% of all trading days, resulted in missing out on 95% of the market's gains.

- From 1963 through 1993, missing the 10 best days lowered the annual return to 10.17% compared to 11.83% for buy-and-hold. But missing the worst 10 days improved the annual return to 14.06%.

- From 1963 through 1993, missing the 90 best days lowered the annual return to 3.28% compared to 11.83% for buy-and-hold. But missing the worst 90 days improved the annual return to 23.0%.

Will Hepburn of Cambridge Investment Research conducted additional research on the "best and worst" days. According to The Society of Asset Allocators and Fund Timers (SAAFTI), Hepburn analyzed the best and worst days data from April 1, 1984, through December 31, 2001 (see Table 2-2). During that time frame the S&P 500 Index gained an annual average 10.35%.

TABLE 2-2

Missing the Best and Worst Days
April 1, 1984, through December 31, 2001

Number of Days	Miss Best Days	Miss Worst Days	Miss Best and Worst Days
10	8.24%	16.55%	13.25%
20	6.09%	19.12%	13.49%
30	4.30%	21.21%	13.53%
40	2.69%	23.15%	13.57%

Source: SAAFTI

Clearly, that analysis also indicates that missing the worst days is preferable to missing the best days as far as improving overall annual returns are concerned. Interestingly, missing the worst *AND* best days still beats the buy-and-hold strategy by 3 percentage points a year.

On November 5, 2001, *Barron's* published an article titled "The Truth About Timing" by Jacqueline Doherty, which is based on a study of the five best and worst days by Birinyi Associates. The investment research firm evaluated the 35-year performance of the S&P 500 Index from 1966 through October 29, 2001, on an annual return basis each year (buy-and-hold), compared to missing the five best and worst days each year.

A $1 investment at the beginning of the period held until the end of the period was worth $11.71 (a 1071 per-cent gain in 35 yrs). But missing just the five best days each year resulted in an astonishing ending value of $0.15 (an 85% loss), compared to a mind-boggling $987.12 (a 98,612% rise) by missing the worst five days each year.

This study sheds a new light on the argument that missing the best days is more important than missing the worst days. It's amazing that 5 days out of 250 in the trading year, or 2% of the trading days a year, can have such a dramatic impact on the annual and compounded performance of investing. That is another reason why an investor should try to minimize his time in the market so that bad things do not happen to good people.

Common Sense Conclusion

I visited the Edward Jones training center for new recruits in 2008. A complete chapter could be filled with this disheartening experience. But I will just say this: Their company slogan is "Making Sense of Investing." Their strategy and sales pitch is "Buy good-quality investments and hold them for a long period of time."

With all their sales strategies, recruiting new sales people, and especially the sales tactics I witnessed, there was NOTHING that "made sense of investing." Investing was the least of concerns. Sales were the one and only concern. New classes of recruits are turned out every week with sales quotas to meet that have absolutely nothing to do with protecting the capital of the investor.

Conversely, while watching CNBC on December 16, 2002, I saw an interview with Vern Hayden, Certified Financial Planner at Hayden Financial Group, when he said that buy-and-hold was no longer a viable strategy. He suggested that investors diversify their holdings and do their own asset allocation. I was encouraged to hear a financial advisor say this on the air. One can hope that he will not be the only voice of sanity on the airwaves in the future.

Buy-and-hold is a great strategy during long-term (secular) bull markets, but it is a very poor strategy during the secular bear markets, where loss of principal can be extensive while inflation eats away at what's left. And as we have seen, these secular bull and bear markets last for many years.

Since history shows that bear markets follow bull markets, then it only makes good sense to sell at the end of the bull market, and put your money into money funds or other safe investment vehicles until the bear market is over. Alternatively you may wish to short the market by shorting with exchange-traded funds or by using inverse funds. These funds specialize in bear market trading.

If investors were to sit down and really think about the frequency of bull and bear market cycles, then they would realize that their inaction (for example, adopting a buy-and-hold strategy) is not an intelligent move at all. Therefore, the only other choice is to have a solid investment plan for investing in the market.

Can you make money Day Trading? Probably not. Very few individuals do. Common Sense Investing is not about attempting to Day Trade the Market, or teach you how to Day Trade.

CHAPTER EIGHT

Common Sense Investing

What You Need to Know

"An investor needs to do very few things right as long as he or she avoids big mistakes."

~Warren Buffett

"Learn how to make money in bear markets, bull markets, and chicken markets."

~Conrad W. Thomas

If you were to mention the words '*Selling at the end of a Bear Market'* in a discussion with your broker or financial advisor, you would probably see the conversation go downhill from there in a hurry. He or she would likely tell you out-right that you cannot be successful trying to move in and out of the market.

If you were to ask these people why they feel that way, they might cite a few academic studies performed a few years ago, that have brought them to that conclusion. Or they might cite some statistics showing that over every 20-year rolling time period, the market has never gone down. However, you can most likely look at the 'Bottom Line" on your investing account statement and see rather quickly the market *DOES* in fact go down.

Even if that were true and over 20 year periods of time the market hasn't gone down, you can't wait for twenty years or more to finally see your money come back from bear market lows. Long-term results cannot help you invest for the here and now, which is when you need to see your money grow.

These types of statistics are so darn misleading.

First of all, you and I both know the market HAS gone down in the past 20 years. There is a reason the magic number of '20 year' is chosen for the illustration.

Secondly, individual stocks and Mutual Funds that invest in those stocks go down and may or may not recover and the individual investor suffers every time this happens.

What is Common Sense Investing?

In general, Common Sense Investing is a strategy that endeavors to be fully invested in the market when it is advancing and to be all in cash or to be short when the market is declining. And that is what is different about Common Sense Investing, compared to buy-and-hold. Of course, this definition applies to investing in any investment vehicle whether it is individual stocks, mutual funds, options, futures, gold or bonds. But most individuals and professionals alike use mutual funds and/or exchange-traded funds as their investment vehicle. Since the stock market has widely outperformed other investment assets such as bonds, gold, and cash, over the long term, investors normally concentrate on the price movements of stocks rather than any other investment choices.

Unfortunately, bear markets intercede every three or four years and cause investors to experience portfolio deterioration.

Remember the Three VERY IMPORTANT bits of investing history?

An analysis of the DJIA from 1885 through 1993:

4. **Found that bear markets consumed 32% of the time of your investment**
5. **Getting back to breakeven took another 44% of the time**
6. **Only 24% of the time was spent in net bull market territory.**

That's the problem when you buy-and-hold. Long periods of negative or zero returns are spent waiting to see how low your investment will go and if you will break even again. And we haven't even factored in the opportunity cost of funds or the ravages of inflation.

The three main objectives of Common Sense Investing are:

- **First and foremost, to preserve your capital**
- **Second, to absolutely evade and avoid large market down-turns, and**
- **Third, to equal or exceed the performance of a buy-and-hold portfolio on a risk-adjusted basis.**

The whole concept is dependent upon limiting the risk when the market begins to decline by going into cash or going short the market. Picture this. If you were in a leaking boat you'd have three choices:

1. **Stay in the boat and stop the leak = Go short.**

2. **Get out of the boat = Switch to cash.**

3. Go down with the ship = Buy-and-hold.

Do I have to ask you which is the worst choice? It's really easy to understand. What's not so easy is to execute. But we'll get to that later in the book.

When you buy-and-hold you are exposing 100% of the invested dollars to market risk 100% of the time. If an investor purchases a mutual fund for $50 a share, uses a buy-and-hold strategy, and then watches as the share price falls to $5 over a three-year time frame, the investor has lost 90% of his or her money. A Common Sense Investing approach would have gotten the investor out of the mutual fund at a much higher price and placed his proceeds of the sale in a money market or T-bill during the downdraft. Thus the risk is reduced, because the time he was invested in the mutual fund is reduced. That is what this is about - reducing your risk.

Classic Common Sense Investors

There are two types of investors: the Classic Market Investor and the Dynamic Asset Allocators.

Classic Investors are the most common and use the simple strategies of Common Sense Investing, usually invest in mutual funds when they are invested in the market, and they move their money into a money market fund or T-bills when they are not invested in the market. They may decide to go from a cash position to a 100% invested position or possibly to a 25% invested position, or in 25% increments, until fully invested, based upon the 'Health' of the market and the economy at the time.

And they may decide to exit the same way, by selling 25% of the investment, in 25% increments. Also, some may go short instead of going into cash, to take full advantage of a market decline. Those who go short the market may also use leveraged funds or they may use unleveraged funds.

Dynamic Asset Allocators

Dynamic Asset Allocators, unlike Classic Investors, are always 100% invested in some asset class, but they spread their investments among stocks, bonds, gold, and cash in varying percentages. They either invest directly in those instruments or they use index funds, sector funds, leveraged funds, or exchange-traded funds that represent those asset classes. For those investors who prefer to always be invested with wide diversification, the asset allocation approach fits the bill nicely. And typically the overall risk of the portfolio is less than investing in one specific investment vehicle such as equities.

Key Points - Using Common Sense

You should understand the following six points about Common Sense Investing:

1. **Common Sense Investing has nothing to do with forecasting the market's future direction**. Samuel Goldwyn once said, "Never make forecasts, especially about the future."

2. **Common Sense Investing assumes that stock prices are not random and that the stock market is not efficient**.

These anomalies allow you to take advantage of trends in the market.

3. **Common Sense Investing should be a mechanical, emotionless approach to investing**. Therefore, once you've decided to use a specific strategy that fits your specific temperament, take *all* the signals and monitor your performance. Once a signal is given, take it and then get ready for the next one. If the last trade was a loss, so be it. Cut your losses short and let your profits run. Small losses are good. But large losses are the killers.

4. **With Common Sense Investing you may underperform in a sustained bull market**. This outcome is to be expected, if the strategy you select has periodic sell signals in an up-trending market. But with Common Sense Investing you will hit the gravy train in bear markets.

5. **Common Sense Investing is not magic, is not 100% accurate, and is not for everyone**. But the strategies have all worked in the past. They are all based on simple strategies, not complicated mathematical equations with numerous variables.

There are no magic rules to follow that will guarantee success, there never has been. Trading programs that advertise to help make trading decisions and trade for you are not magic either. If it were that easy, everyone would be wealthy, no one would ever lose money, and the software developers would be even wealthier since they would own the 'Goose that laid the Golden Egg'.

What does work is having your investing plan and following it.

"I measure what's going on, and I adapt to it. I try to get my ego out of the way. The market is smarter than I am so I bend"
~Martin Zweig

Common Sense Conclusion

You know, being a wise investor is not easy. But if you have the Common Sense to ignore the Talking Heads on TV and trash any sales brochures you receive on investing opportunities, then you are well on your way to success.

For example: In the December 30, 2002 *Barron's* article. Ten well-known market strategists from leading firms were interviewed and asked for their market predictions for the upcoming year. Nine out of ten predicted a rising market. And only one predicted a drop, but he was off by 75 S&P 500 points. He predicted a close of 950 on the S&P 500, but it actually closed at 875.

When hearing some misleading statistics about ***20 year rolling time periods***, it simply makes my skin crawl. Why not 15 year periods, or 18 year periods? Why pick 20 year? Obviously, during Secular Bear Markets there have been 15 and 18 year periods when there was little or no gain. So, choosing 20 year periods conveniently makes the numbers sound better. Investors should be told the truth, that yes, there are many times if you simply hold an investment there may be no gain.

When presented with this, simply ask that Advisor if the same advice was given in 2000, or in 2007. Someone bought those stocks at the top of the market. And what about the 25 year period investors waited to break even from 1929 to 1954?

Another thing to always remember is this: It ALWAYS depends on when you buy the investment. As you learned, during a Secular Bear Market, if you purchased at or near a high, then you could be forced to hold the investment for many years before breaking even.

As far as statistics go:

"Statistics are like bikinis. What they reveal is suggestive, but what they conceal is vital."

CHAPTER NINE

Choosing an Investment Vehicle

"Indexing is the best approach to the stock market for 99% of all investors." ~Warren Buffett

Deciding what to invest in is critical. Selecting a good investment vehicle that blends well with your style of investing is imperative. Most Common Sense Investors do not invest in individual stocks. Individual stocks expose the investor to too much risk.

To successfully pick stocks that make you money is not easy because the odds are heavily stacked against you. Another difficulty is determining exactly when to buy and sell your stocks. Moreover, if your stock portfolio is not diversified, you may be inadvertently exposing yourself to more risk than you intended to take.

Bad news about your stock, its industry group, or even a competitor's stock can result in large down moves, and it can decimate your stock's price by 25 to 50% almost overnight. To avoid potential losses that can occur at any time for any reason, the astute investor will steer clear of individual securities entirely. Simply put, the risks are too high with respect to the rewards. If the vast majority of professional money managers with the financial credentials and experience cannot consistently pick a stock portfolio that does better than a comparable benchmark index, then how do you expect to do it?

Instead of investing in individual stocks, consider investing in a portfolio of diversified mutual funds: these could be index funds, sector funds, and exchange-traded funds which represent a wide range of indexes. You should understand each of these investment vehicles, and then you need to decide for yourself which ones you feel comfortable investing in, based upon your risk tolerance. This chapter will cover the basics on index, sector, and leveraged funds, while the next chapter covers exchange-traded funds.

What about Mutual Funds?

Mutual Funds are one of the most popular ways to invest. They desperately want to manage your money for you. Besides, they all have Fund managers, researchers, Analysts, Salespeople, secretaries, offices, and high-rises. They must know what there're doing, right? But who pays for all of that? Yes, you, the investor.

When you invest in a Mutual Fund, you are likely paying a fee up front, which will immediately decrease the amount of your investment. Then you will only make money on your investment if the Fund increases in value over and above the amount necessary to pay the continuing fees to support all the personnel and other expenses involved.

Do Mutual Funds really make money?

Some do, many don't.

- 75% of Funds with a 1 star rating in 2005 were wiped out during the next 5 years.
- There were 650 funds with Growth in their names that actually shrunk over the 2000- 2010 decade.

- 7.54% of funds with the word Plus in their names have underperformed during the 2000-2010 decade.

According to Morningstar who rates Mutual Funds as to their performance, as of October 1st, 2010:

The bottom line:
Group average total return updated daily by Morningstar:

10,971 Mutual Funds 5 year total return =	2.87
13,534 Mutual Funds 3 year total return =	-2.70
15,942 Mutual Funds Year to Date return =	6.51

Source: Morningstar.com

Point is, in order to make an informed decision you must look at a performance history of the fund. A long-term history will show you how the Fund actually performed during good times and bad.

But look at it logically. How is the performance of a Mutual Fund Rated? The performance of the S&P 500 Index is used as the **Industry Standard Benchmark** to gauge the performance of Mutual Funds.

Therefore if a Mutual Fund outperforms the S&P 500, then it is considered to be performing well. And obviously, underperforming the S&P 500 would be considered 'Not doing so well'.

So realistically, if your Mutual Fund strives to beat the performance of the S&P 500, why not just invest your money in the S&P 500 index by buying shares of **SPY**? In doing so, you avoid paying fees to a 'Fund', Investment Firm, Fund Manager, commissions, etc., and you would have a well diversified investment comprised of 500 of the biggest and best companies in the country. And, the only fees you would pay would be a commission for the trade.

Hardly any of the Mutual Fund managers follow a buy-and-hold strategy for their fund's portfolio. According to Morningstar, who rates Mutual Funds, the average portfolio turnover of a diversified stock Mutual Fund is 115% a year. That means that on average every stock in the Mutual Fund portfolio is sold each year and replaced by new ones. So, if it looks like Common Sense Investing and smells like Common Sense Investing, then it is Common Sense Investing and should be acknowledged as such since it is practiced by Mutual Fund managers whose firms profess holding investments to the individual investor. What's good for the goose should be good for the gander.

Here is another thing about Funds you should be aware of. Have you ever heard the term 'Window Dressing'? As it relates to investing and Stock market Lingo, and not referring to the little dress shop on the downtown square. Do you ever pay much attention to the information you receive from your Investment Firm? Particularly what your Fund has invested your money in. This is where the term 'Window Dressing' comes from.

You see, about 2 to 5 days right before the firms prepare the information to be sent out to their investors, there is always a noticeable volatility in trading. This is due to the Firms selling and unloading the bad investments they made and purchasing other investments that are currently doing well. This 'Dresses' up the appearance of the information you receive, and is an effort to lead you to believe you are invested in really profitable companies. Well, maybe you are, now! But the recent advance in the price of some of those companies didn't really help the bottom line on your statement since the purchase was only made by the Firm 2 or 3 days ago. You can do better.

Active Investing using Leveraged Funds:

Be Very Careful

Using leveraged funds and making a lot of money is the ultimate goal for seasoned active investors. Initially, investors just starting out may not want to jump right into leveraged funds. Until the investor feels comfortable with his investing plan, his rules for cutting loses, including the use of stop-loss orders, the use of leveraged funds, should probably be avoided. A novice investor using leverage can get destroyed if the market turns against him, and if he does not get out immediately with a small loss.

Losses of 50% and higher can easily occur using leveraged funds if a trading plan is not implemented precisely.

Common Sense Conclusion

After investors have actively invested profitably for a few years they may want to consider investing in leveraged funds, but only with the minimal account size, at the beginning. After six months, more funds can be added. Slow and steady wins the race with these enhanced funds. Your main concern is minimizing your losses and protecting your capital, NOT maximizing your profits.

That gain will come, it is hoped, if you have the proper investing plan in place and if you follow your plan. Leveraged funds offer investors who get on the right side of the market a powerful vehicle for participating in both bull and bear markets. For aggressive investors who are able to control their risk, leveraged funds can lead to tremendous returns. Of course, more reward means more risk.

CHAPTER TEN

Exchange Traded Funds - ETFs

The investment vehicle of choice for many active investors using Common Sense Investing, are Exchange Traded Funds.

ETF BASICS

Exchange-traded funds (ETFs) are commonly used for trading and investing by active investors and traders, not buy-and-hold investors. As investors become more familiar with the characteristics of ETFs, they will draw assets away from conventional mutual funds and index funds.

In the United States, there are about 125 ETFs valued at well over $100 billion, representing popular indexes, international indexes, and various sectors of the market. Almost all ETFs are listed on the American Stock Exchange (AMEX), except for three international ETFs listed on the NYSE and two listed on the Nasdaq. A listing of AMEX-listed ETFs can be found at *www.amex.com*, along with other useful information.

According to the AMEX, the official definition of ETFs is "registered investment companies under the Investment Company Act of 1940, which have received certain exceptive relief from the SEC to allow secondary market trading in the ETF shares. ETFs are index-based products, in that each ETF holds a portfolio of securities that is intended to provide investment results that, before fees and expenses, generally correspond to the price and yield performance of the underlying benchmark index."

In 1993, the AMEX listed the first ETF: the Standard & Poor's Depositary Receipt (SPDR), pronounced "spider." It exactly mirrors the movement of the S&P 500 Index. Its ticker symbol is **SPY**. There are also ETFs that track the DJIA, called "Diamonds", ticker symbol **DIA**; the Nasdaq 100 (**QQQ**), called "Cubes"; the largest 1000 U.S. incorporated companies, known as the Russell 1000 (**IWB**); and many other industry sectors and indexes.

The most heavily traded ETFs are as follows:

SPY. SPDR Trust Series securities, SPDRs: Pooled investments that track the price and yield of the S&P 500 Index.

QQQ. The Nasdaq-100 Trust Series I: A pooled investment that tracks the price and yield of the Nasdaq 100 Index.

DIA. Diamonds Trust Series I: A pooled investment that tracks the price and yield of the DJIA.

MDY. SPDR Trust series: S&P 400 Mid-cap.

iSHARES. Pooled-securities with an open-ended investment structure issued by Barclays Global Investors. There are over 50 different iShares index funds that trade like stocks. Each share tracks a specific portfolio. For a complete description, check out the iShares Web site at *www.ishares.com*.

Active Investing using ETFs

ETFs offer advantages over mutual funds and index funds that make them more attractive and liquid for the active investor. ETFs are diversified. Investors can be more aggressive and buy and sell industry-sector ETFs. And ETFs are a great tool to develop a balanced investment portfolio because of the array of choices.

However, ETFs are not leveraged, so an investor would have to use a margin account through his or her broker to obtain leverage and incur margin interest until the ETF position is closed.

The most popular ETFs to use for Common Sense Investing are the QQQs, SPYs, and DIAs. They each have huge trading volume, offer minimal bid/ask spreads, and represent a very significant specific market segment.

Common Sense Conclusion

ETFs are great investment vehicles that offer outstanding flexibility and a wide range of options. An investment plan can be easily implemented with these hybrid mutual funds. Best of all, ETFs can be bought and sold any time throughout the day, and they can be easily shorted. But if you want to leverage ETFs, you'll only need to open a margin account and pay the margin interest on any trade or investment that you wish to use 'leverage' on.

CHAPTER ELEVEN

Indicators

Indicators to Determine the Market's Health

Using Common Sense Investing obviously does not include buying something and forgetting about it. Holding an investment and hoping for the best is in no way using common sense, and can put you in the fast lane to financial ruin. **Investing successfully always requires being on the right side of the market.** Formulating an Investment Plan requires putting the odds in your favor, and to do this, the intelligent investor uses the necessary available tools.

Let's start with indicators. Market indicators give us a window to view what is really happening with the market, and also helps eliminate the 'noise'. By having a clear picture of what the market is doing you can formulate an investing plan that is far more likely to be successful.

Wouldn't it be great to be able to discern the market's current well-being so that you could detect a change in the trend? And wouldn't you like to be able to accomplish this feat yourself without having to rely on the advice of any investment newsletter subscription or the Talking Heads on Wall Street? Well, believe it or not, you can determine when a change in direction will likely occur, if you know what to look for and where to look. The market signals its health to those who know how to read its vital signs.

The 'Health" of the overall market is of major importance. Remember, all ships rise and fall with the tide. It *DOES NOT* matter if you pick the best stock or the best Mutual Fund on the Planet, if the general market is headed down, they will follow.

To determine the market's current "health," you need to analyze specific data that reveals the market's most probable condition. That is why it is necessary to find specific indicators that have a high degree of accuracy over a long period of time that provide guidance on the market's health and potential future direction. There are hundreds of stock market statistics and indicators that can be used to monitor the stock market's health. But the vast majority of them either fail to provide the information that we are looking for or they do not have a high degree of historical reliability.

WHAT AN INDICATOR MUST SHOW US

Our objective is, first, to determine whether the market is in a major trend (up or down) or in a "trading range" where the price vacillates back and forth between two price levels, essentially going sideways. Second, we want to know if the market is in an extremely "over-bought" or "oversold" condition. An "overbought" market is one in which the market indices are at such a high price level that individual investors and market professionals are exuberantly bullish. This condition can go on for an extended period of time, as indicated by the market's huge run-up from October 1999 through March 2000, and from the lows in March 2003 through the highs in July 2003, or the run-up in 2007.

On the other hand, when the market is "oversold," it is at such a low price level that individual investors and market professionals are excessively bearish. This is when no one wants to own a share of stock, and is scared to buy one. This condition can also go on for some time before a change in trend occurs. It is critical for investors to be investing with the major trend and **NOT against it**. That is why investors have to stay alert to an impending change in the market's direction.

No one can determine exactly where and when the market will change direction but what you want to look for are indications that the market is at an extremely high or low price level, and I want to emphasize EXTREME, because when that occurs, the market usually reverses in the opposite direction.

If we, as investors, can take advantage of that situation, then we are well on our way to investing profitably. That's why we need to take the pulse of the market to determine if it's healthy and headed upward, or if it is weak and headed downward. Either of these conditions can be turned to your advantage if you put yourself on the right side of the market's new direction.

First, we will focus on sentiment indicators that measure the psychological framework of investors and professionals as well. Second, we will focus on the internal market indicators that mea-sure the market's strength or weakness.

These Indicators are usually reliable in showing the condition of the market, and you should check these indicators weekly. However, during market extremes such as January 2000, September 2001, July and October 2002, March and July 2003, and August 2007 and March 2009, they should be checked daily so that you can ascertain a better entry/exit point for your investments. In the case of all the indicators in this chapter, it is imperative to wait until the extreme reading for each specific indicator is *reversed* and the indicator begins to change direction. By acting early and not waiting for this important reversal signal, you risk the market continuing to go in its current direction for days, weeks, or months at a time.

The following (Figure 8-1) is an example of the Extreme.

Figure 8-1

The above is a 5-year chart of the DJIA with a 200 Day Moving Average displayed as the single line.

This chart shows both of the extremes, the all-time high for the DJIA in 2007 and the low of 2009. This particular chart will reveal much more, later in the book. But for now, you should realize that an all-time high most always has a tendency to be an 'extreme', and obviously a low that is more than 50% less than the previous high would also be an 'extreme.'

Just a side NOTE: What if you had sold at the top in 2007 and bought back at the bottom in 2009? Would your portfolio look drastically better? Then keep reading.

DETERMINE THE CONSENSUS OPINION

> "**Be fearful when others are greedy and greedy only when others are fearful.**" *~Warren Buffett*

Using a Contrarian approach can be helpful for a couple of reasons. Sentiment measurements are useful in determining the opinion, not only of the average investor but also of the professional investment advisors and money managers. By watching the latest market calls of these market participants, and investing in the opposite direction (only during market extremes), you can become a more profitable investor. Since the consensus opinion, whether among the average investors or professionals, is usually, but not always, wrong at *extremes*, you can pinpoint the most advantageous and low-risk entry/exit points at which to invest.

Index of Investor Optimism:
Another Contrary Sentiment Indicator

The Index of Investor Optimism measures the opinions of individual investors. When this indicator is at its low and high points it has signaled the market's major turning points very well. Started in October 1996, this survey is conducted monthly by Gallup. Approximately 1000 different randomly selected investors with over $10,000 in investments from across the country are surveyed each month, to assess their level of optimism or pessimism about the stock market.

For an example, figure 4-2 below, shows the index readings since inception through December 2002. As you can see, 178 was the highest reading of investor optimism, in January 2000—right at the market top for the DJIA. The previous peak in readings came in April 1999 at 168, again another high point in the market averages. Another high reading was in August 2000 at 160.

FIGURE 4-2

Index of Investor Optimism® October 1996–December 2002

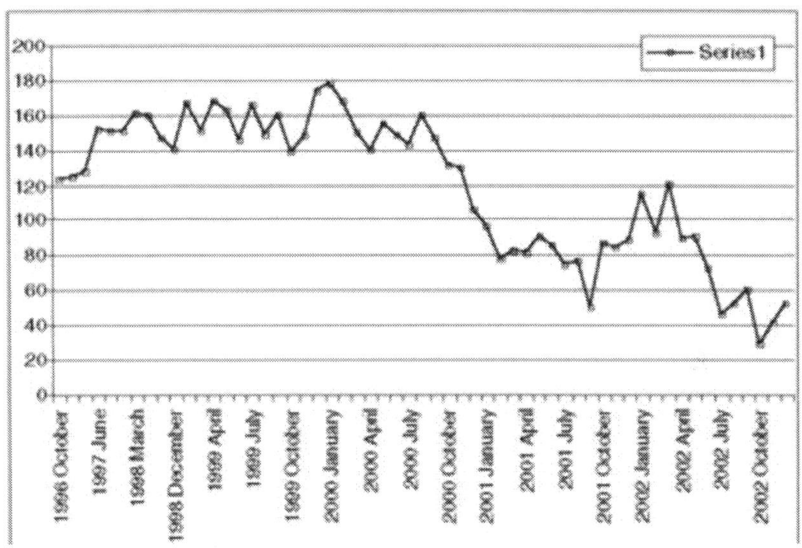

The lowest readings of the Index of Investor Optimism since inception have occurred at the lowest points of the market. In October 2002 at 29 when the market hit a major low on October 9, 2002, and the survey was performed between October 1 and 17.

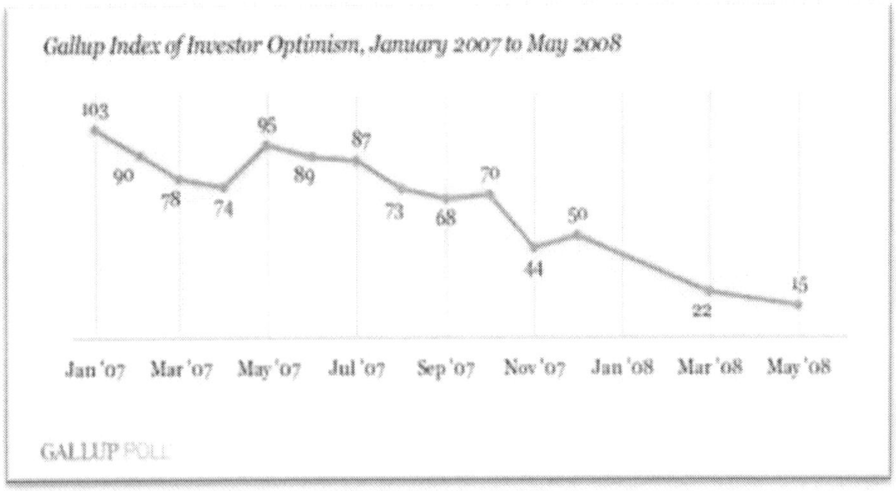

Notice the high reading of 103 in January 2007 while the market was topping out again, and the low of 15 by May of 2008 during the bear market.

What this index tells us is that investors were the most optimistic about the stock market when prices were at their highest. Is the opposite true, that when the market is at very low points, investor optimism is at a low point? Absolutely!

As I said, this index should be interpreted as a **contrary indicator**. Meaning simply, when investors are very optimistic as indicated by high readings, then that is the time to consider going into cash, or to shorting the market. And when investors are very pessimistic when readings are low, then that is a good time to consider buying, or at least begin looking for opportunities.

This indicator should not be used by itself to make buy or sell decisions but should be used in conjunction with the other internal market indicators. In this way you are able to wait for confirmation of the future direction of the market taken from all of the indicators you are observing.

CBOE Options Volatility Index (VIX): The Investor Fear Gauge

Some investors watch for high readings on the VIX (Options Volatility Index) and the VXN. The VIX and the VXN measure the expectations of options traders who buy and sell the options of stocks traded on the NYSE and Nasdaq, respectively. The options themselves are traded on the Chicago Board of Options Exchange (CBOE).

According to their Web site *www.cboe.com:* VIX and VXN provide investors with up-to-the-minute market estimates of expected volatility by using real-time index option bid/ask quotes. The CBOE VIX and VXN index prices are both designed to reflect the implied volatilities of certain index options contracts; VIX is based on the prices of eight S&P 100 (OEX) index puts and calls, while VXN is based on the prices of Nasdaq 100 (NDX) options prices.

High and Low Readings of VIX

High VIX readings indicate fear among investors who are purchasing significantly more Put options than Call options.

Put options are bets that the market will fall while Call options are bets in anticipation of a market rise. There is a high correlation between high VIX readings and the occurrence of market bottoms. When this indicator is at high readings, and options buyers are scared, then that is bullish. So there is an inverse relationship between the extreme reading and its meaning. Again wait for a reversal or confirmation from other indicators before investing.

Low readings of VIX do not have the same significance and should not be taken to mean that stock prices will fall. The low readings tend to be more reactive than predictive.

Again, these indicators should be used in conjunction with other market indicators, not in isolation.

INTERNAL MARKET INDICATORS

The key to profitable investing is to be on the right side of the market, period. Too many investors do not pay attention to what the market is saying. Instead, they prefer to read financial and investment magazines, newspapers, and newsletters and watch financial shows which transmit the 'Market Hype' instead of the objective facts you need.

These "Spin Stories" are most always sensationalized to get ratings and are very misleading. This means all the information investors receive from these avenues is pretty much worthless, and just "noise." It has no value to the average person as to what he or she needs to know to be a more informed investor.

Instead, every investor should use a more systematic analytical approach and learn to understand what the market itself is telling them to determine if it is time to buy or sell. This goal can be easily accomplished by "putting your ear to the ground" and "listening" carefully to what the market is telling you.

New Highs – New Lows

Besides the previously discussed Contrarian indicators, another indicator that is very significant and accurate is the new Highs-new Lows indicator.

This information is comprised of how many stocks are making new highs and how many are making new lows. For instance, in a healthy market there will consistently be more stocks making new highs than there are stocks making new lows. Again, this is Common Sense. Obviously, this would usually give you the general health of the market even if you had no other information at all.

It is also used as confirmation to what the indexes and averages are saying.

For instance, there are times that the DJIA may be positive and up for the day, the week, or the month, but the new highs and new lows may not confirm a healthy market. In other words, the DJIA may be in positive territory at the same time there are more stocks making new lows than there are making new highs. This conflicting information would be a signal that the market is not healthy. This might also be an indication that money was being moved into the blue chip stocks and out of small caps, mid-caps, etc.

There are other times that there may be more stocks making new highs, yet the indexes and averages may not be doing the same.

There are many reasons why at times the new highs and new lows do not coincide with the major averages and indexes. If you will remember prior to the bear market 2000-2002, the blue chips, and the DJIA in particular, were the last sector to advance.

Of course the talking heads claimed that the advance in the blue chips at that time was simply, **"They are just catching up with the tech stocks"**. But as the blue chips advanced there was very little advance in technology stocks. This indicates that money was being moved out of technology and into 'Safety', the blue chips.

Common Sense Investing uses the new highs and new lows to get a general pulse of the market and to confirm what the major averages may be doing. New highs and new lows should never be used as the only indicator in deciding to enter or exit the market. The general pulse of the market obtained by the new highs and new lows should be used in conjunction with the moving averages that we discuss later.

Another very good indicator that is a 'Rule of Thumb' to use is the NYSE Composite Index. The NYSE Composite is a stock market index covering all common stock listed on the New York Stock Exchange, including American Depositary Receipts, Real Estate Investment Trusts, tracking stocks, and foreign listings. If the market is weak, then there are times this index will alert you.

The following table is an excellent example of an early alert of market weakness.

▾ Quotes - Edit

Symbol	Price	Change	
DJIA	11,146.57	+38.60	+0.35%
^NYA	7,515.67	-8.14	-0.11%
S&P 500	1,180.26	+2.09	+0.18%
NASDAQ	2,459.67	+2.28	+0.09%

The above table was captured early in the day showing the DJIA, S&P500, and the Nasdaq all in positive territory. On the surface, it appears the market is advancing nicely, right? Wrong. The NYSE Composite Index was down. This indicates that only selected stocks are higher, and the broader market is showing signs of weakness.

The following table was later the very same day.

Last update: 01:25 pm CDT - Refresh

▾ Quotes - Edit

Symbol	Price	Change	
DJIA	11,089.20	-18.77	-0.17%
^NYA	7,474.30	-49.51	-0.66%
S&P 500	1,173.38	-4.79	-0.41%
NASDAQ	2,440.94	-16.45	-0.67%

As you can see, the market wasn't as healthy as it might have first appeared.

Percentage of Stocks above their 200-Day Moving Average

Another indicator that can be helpful in determining the health of the market is the percentage of stocks above the 200 DMA.

Shown below in Figure 8-4 is a chart of the NYSE Composite Index on the upper graph and the percentage of stocks above their 200-dma on the lower graph. The 200-dma is a long-term moving average; stocks tend to stay above or below it for extended periods during bull or bear runs.

Figure 8-4

Percent of NYSE Stocks Above Their 200-Day Moving Averages

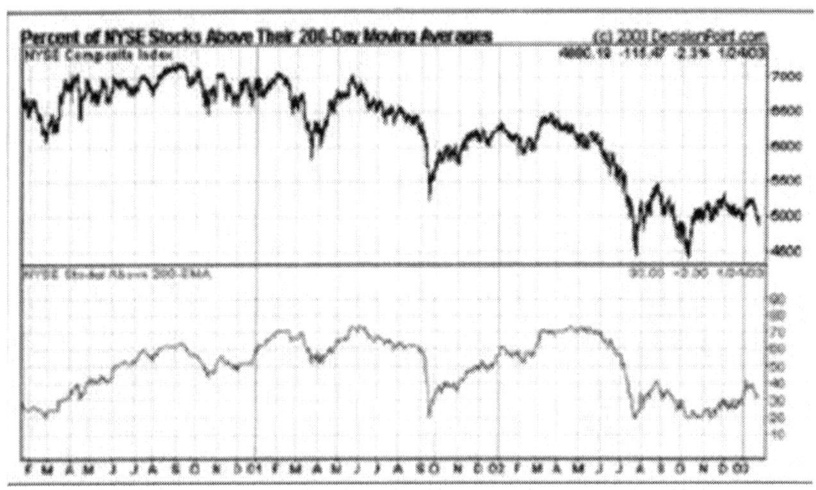

This indicator not only shows when the market is healthy, it can also be a Contrarian Indicator. Meaning, when the market becomes over-bought and/or peaks, you will find that 70% or more of all stocks on the NYSE trade above their own 200 DMA.

These situations occurred in February 2001, May and June 2001, and March through June 2002 and again in 2007 as the market was topping out.

When the market reaches a bottom or is over-sold you will find that only about 20% of all stocks are trading above their 200-dma.

When the market finally hit bottom on October 9, 2002, only about 20% of stocks were trading above their 200 DMA.

Another thing to always watch for is a false rally. For instance, on November 6, 2002 the market was up. The DJIA was up 20.4% and the Nasdaq Composite Index was up 27.4%. But the percentage of stocks above their 200 DMA was only 25%. This signaled a very weak advance from the low 20% level. Meaning simply, that most stocks were not really making much progress even though the market rally was quick and substantial off the bottom. So this was not a positive sign of strength. The indicator peaked at around 43% in the first few days of 2003 but then turned down again to near 30 while the market went down.

Remember, if you use a shorter time frame such as a 20 DMA or 50 DMA the number of buy and sell signals will be more frequent, and there may be many more false signals given. You won't realize that you received a false signal until after the fact, so it's a good idea to confirm it with other indicators. So, be careful using these time frames. You should also wait for the extreme reading to reverse before investing.

Common Sense Conclusion

The market speaks loudly and clearly, just like the Talking Heads. Your goal is to learn 'WHO' to listen to. And obviously, the market is the only one that matters. The market is always right, and if you listen, it will give you valuable clues as to whether it is healthy or not. This solid information is very useful in helping you determine whether the market has reached a low or high point. That information alone is very useful in making your investment decisions. By combining the internal market indicators with the previously discussed sentiment indicators, you will be on the right side of the market more often than not.

Before you decide to risk your money and buy a stock or invest in a fund, you should always decide the general direction of the market and whether it is healthy or if it is showing signs of weakness. This will keep your money out of danger most of the time.

For instance, just like the Exchange Composite tables above. If you were going to invest that day and saw the composite was weak, you would have waited until a better time. And later that that proved your decision to wait would have been correct. Without checking the composite, you would have bought early that day and watched your investment decline immediately.

C H A P T E R TWELVE

Investing Strategies

"The only thing that works is to let the market indices tell you the time to enter and exit. Never fight the market—it's bigger than you are."
~*William J. O'Neil,* How to Make Money in Stocks

Every Investor must have a plan, a strategy, and a way to invest other than relying on others or sticking your head in the sand and hoping for the best. As you have seen, those methods are not highly profitable.

Two strategies that have proven effective over time are "Calendar-Based Investing" and "The Best Six Months Strategy". We'll begin with them.

Calendar-Based Investing

BACKGROUND

Investing based on using the calendar has intrigued investors, market technicians, and other investment professionals for years. For the most part, the broadcast media has mentioned seasonal investing strategies on occasion, but they have not given it the attention it deserves. Therefore, most investors may have heard something about it but not taken it seriously or done any homework on the topic. As it turns out, that lack of initiative was probably a huge mistake, because careful analysis of seasonal investing strategies reveals their superiority to buy-and-hold over a long time period.

Over the years, many academic studies have been done on the seasonal influences on stock market returns. *Calendar Based* and *Best Six Months Strategies* are profitable strategies that have not only worked in the past, but also in the present. Excluding the worst-performing months, staying out of the market and into cash, is an excellent strategy. It not only reduces risk but also provides better-than-average risk-adjusted returns.

Investing during specific months each year is an example of a seasonality pattern. According to *The Wall Street Journal*, Ned Davis Research found that since 1950, on average, stocks have gone up 8% from the beginning of October through the end of April but have increased only 1% from the beginning of May through the end of September.

That firm found that investing $10,000 from the fourth trading day in May, through the last trading day in September of the following year (or a continuous period of 6 months), from 1950 through 2000, resulted in a miniscule total gain of $2977 for that entire period. However, entering into the market every October 1 and exiting the following May 3 resulted in a total gain of $585,909.

Look at Table 8-1 to get a better idea as to the best-performing consecutive months. Note that the period November through January offers the highest return compared to any other three consecutive months.

TABLE 8.1

Best Consecutive Three-Month Periods For S&P 500 Index

[average cumulative change 1928–2002 (Oct.)]

Period	Change, %
Nov., Dec., Jan.	3.8
June, July, Aug.	3.5
Dec., Jan., Feb.	3.1
Oct., Nov., Dec.	2.5
Average 3 months	1.8

SO, WHAT SHOULD YOU DO?

Investing is a serious business, not a game. You can't make money at it if you're going to invest your money on a whim, or on a tip you heard at the office water cooler. You need to go with the highest performance probabilities that have been proven from the past and never fall into the trap that, this time it will be different.

Let's look at it logically and realistically. History tells us a lot.

HISTORICAL PERSPECTIVE

The individual monthly performance of the S&P 500 Index over the past 50 years is depicted in Table 8-2. This table provides the monthly performance of the S&P 500 Index from 1950 through March 2002, divided into two time frames. Clearly there are specific strong and weak months. January, April, July, November, and December have been the best-performing months from 1950 through 1995. Excluding July, *the continuous months of November through January are the best ones*, with an average gain of 1.58% per month. By including February, March, and April, the performance falls to 1.19%, but it is still positive.

TABLE 8.2

Monthly Performance of S&P 500
S&P 500 Monthly Prices
1950–March 2002

	Average Monthly Gain, %		
Month	**1950–1995**	**1996–Mar. 2002**	**Difference**
January	**1.55**	**1.31**	−0.24
February	0.37	−0.87	−1.24
March	0.76	**1.76**	1.00
April	**1.23**	**2.75**	1.51
May	0.16	0.35	0.19
June	0.08	**2.31**	**2.22**
July	**1.29**	−0.63	−1.92
August	0.39	−3.24	−3.63
September	−0.60	−0.15	0.45
October	0.45	**2.64**	**2.19**
November	**1.43**	**3.50**	**2.07**
December	**1.77**	**1.77**	0
Average	0.74	0.95	0.21
Nov.–Jan. only	**1.58**	**2.14**	0.56
Nov.–Apr. only	1.19	**1.63**	0.44
May–Oct. only	0.29	0.21	−0.08

Note: Bolded numbers are the best performing monthly.

Now let's look at the more recent time period, from 1996 to March 2002 in Table 8.2. The best-performing months are January, March, April, June, October, November, and December. March, June, and October have now emerged as strong months.

The five months including March, April, June, October, and November have provided higher performance in the most recent six-year period compared to the prior period. Except for June, these are all months in the October to April time frame.

History clearly indicates that there is consistently a period of strong and weak months. There are many probable reasons for this. For instance: Traders, investors, money managers, and most potential 'Buyers' are the ones that drive the market higher. Their buying is somewhat curtailed while they are vacationing during the summer months. That is why many refer to the summer as the 'Doldrums.' A reason the market might advance in October, November, December time frame is the seasonal buying related to holidays. Many companies have their best performances of the year during this time period, and when the companies have good sales, the income, or the expected income, will show up in their stock prices.

Regardless of the reasons, the investor who wishes to limit 'Market Risk' can take advantage of this strategy, especially in retirement accounts, where there are no capital gains implications for selling and can capitalize on these strong and weak monthly patterns.

Let's take a closer look at the 'Seasonal Strategies'.

Best Six-Month Strategy

There are several reasons investors should consider seasonal patterns besides the fact they have stood the test of time.

The '*Best Six Months Strategy'* has the following characteristics:

- There are only two signals a year - one buy and one sell.
- The buy signal will usually be in October, and the sell signal will usually be in April.
- The annual rate of return exceeds the buy-and-hold strategy, on a risk-adjusted basis.
- This strategy misses the brunt of most bear markets, since you are not invested in the weakest half of the year, but instead, you are invested in the strongest months of the year.
- This strategy provides 50% less risk to your portfolio than buy-and-hold. (50% less time IN the market)
- The time required to implement the strategy is minimal (about an hour a year).

These attributes should get most investors' attention because all the research data over the past 50 years supports it.

Let's take a closer look at the evidence to understand how successful the seasonal investing strategy can be, and why you may want to use it with your hard-earned cash.

Most refer to this Common Sense Approach as a simple "Timing" strategy. But it does have a long-term track-record. It was actually developed in 1986 by Yale Hirsch. It was first published in The Hirsch Organization's 1987 edition of the *Stock Trader's Almanac*. It has been tweaked a bit over the years by his son Jeff Hirsch, and is updated annually in each year's edition of the almanac. Moreover, the BSM's current buy-and-sell signals are provided in real time to subscribers of their monthly newsletter *Stock Trader's Almanac Investor* newsletter, as well as via their subscriber email service.

The BSM strategy's buy-and-sell rules are simple: invest in the stock market (for example, a S&P 500 Index fund) on November 1st of each year, and then sell on April 30th of the following year and go into cash equivalents such as a money fund or T-bills, until November 1st rolls around when the next investment is made.

Clearly, the months selected for investing play a significant role in the total return over that extensive time period. On page 52 of the almanac, the same strategy is tested, but in conjunction with a technical indicator known as the Moving Average Convergence-Divergence (MACD), based on the work of Sy Harding.

Using the MACD's buy signal, you would buy on a date ***near*** November when the market conditions were best, and your sell signal would be ***near*** April when the market conditions were most favorable.

NOTE: The 'MACD' indicator can be added to most any chart found on the internet, even the free ones like Yahoo.

Now look at *WHAT* would you have missed by being *OUT* of the market for 6 months each of those years.

Keep in mind that, for an investor who had been using the BSM strategy, the worst market meltdowns would all have been avoided:

- The October 28 and 29, 1929, crash, in which the DJIA dropped 25.2%

- The October 19, 1987, stock market crash, in which the DJIA plunged over 508 points, dropping 22.6%
- The 555-point drop on October 27, 1997 (–7.2%)
- The 513-point drop on August 31, 1998 (–6.4%)
- The 357-point drop on August 27, 1998 (–4.2%)
- The 1370-point drop between September 10 and 21, 2001 (–14.3%), after the terrorist attack on the World Trade Center and Washington, DC
- The 1651-point, third-quarter 2002 (–17.9%) decline
- The 3733-point DJIA decline in 2008 April 30 – October 30 (-29%)

We will look closer at the 2008 drop in the chapter on moving averages. But, as you can clearly see, even if you missed some of the gains while you were out of the market, your investments would have been far safer to avoid the major declines.

Common Sense Conclusion

The Calendar Based and Best Six Month Strategies have a long history to support and validate their use. Using one of these strategies that fit your personal investing style will likely work well, and protect you capital in the long run.

It is Common Sense really. Historically, seldom are there any gains in the market through the summer months and many of the severe declines and crashes have been in October. So why put your investments at risk when the 'Odds' are not favorable.

Unfavorable odds is like buying a Mutual Fund or Stock and never checking what the market is currently doing, where it has been trading, or showing any concern as to where it might be heading.

The next strategy is the Simple moving Average and how it can make investing simpler than ever.

CHAPTER THIRTEEN

Moving Averages

My Personal Favorite

Yes, Moving Averages are my personal favorite. They work well whether you want to be in the market for long periods of time, short periods of time, or even if you want to Swing Trade the Market. And they are available on virtually any charting software, even the free ones like Yahoo.

Securities prices, market indexes, and mutual fund prices vacillate up and down from day to day, week to week and month to month. Because of this it often becomes difficult to discern which way the prices are actually moving. A moving average is therefore used to smooth the data so that the trend can be easily detected. A rising moving-average line indicates that prices are trending up, while a declining line indicates the opposite. A flat line indicates a market stuck in a trading range that can't seem to make up its mind where it is going.

The following chart (Figure 8-1) is a 5-year chart of the DJIA with a 200 DMA. The Moving average is the solid line shown on the chart.

Figure 8-1

You can create a moving average of any length (e.g., 10-day, 20-day, 50-day, 200-day) and for any time period (days, weeks, months) depending upon what you are trying to achieve: for example, for trading the market over short time frames a short time-frame chart would be used with a short moving average. On the other hand, investing for the long term, a long term chart would be used with longer term moving averages.

Basically, when investing, you want to be ***invested in the market*** when the price of the stock or index crosses above the moving average, and ***out of the market*** or short the market when the price crosses below the moving average. To determine when this happens you would be following the price crossovers of the moving averages for one or more of the major market indexes such as the DJIA, the S&P 500, the Nasdaq 100, the Russell 3000, etc.

Referring to Figure 8-6 below, you can clearly see the concept of using moving averages.

Figure 8-6

When the S&P 500 Index's price crossed below the 200 DMA you would have SOLD and got out of the market on September 25th, 2000, missing the 609-point drop from 1436 to 827 in September 2002. During this period of time, the S&P 500 only penetrated the 200 DMA a couple of times in early 2002. Even if you were anxious to re-invest and hurriedly bought as soon as the index touched the 200 DMA, you would have sold almost immediately when it crossed back over the average.

Some of the more popular time periods used by market professionals for moving average crossovers are the 20-dma, the 50-dma, and the 200-dma. Keep in mind that investing using moving averages for buy and sell signals, it is critical to select an average that is not too sensitive to "whipsaws." Rapid upswings in price above the moving average only to soon reverse and fall below the average, and to downswings which can do the same, first falling below the moving average and then soon turning up above the average. This situation is most common during a market that is trading sideways in a trading range. Also, be aware that the shorter the time period chosen, then the more subject you are to whipsaws and false breakouts. While the longer the time frame you use, the slower the signal, and you will avoid many whipsaws but you may also miss a part of the move that had already begun. So, the time frame you will most likely choose will be relative to whether you are trading with a short-term or a long-term objective.

200 DMA vs. 50 DMA

The 200 DMA is considered the one most indicative that a real market trend is in place because it covers a period of 40 weeks worth of trading. In the next two charts, Figure 8-6 and Figure 8-6a, you can see that the 200 DMA is slower moving and farther away from the prices, while the 50-day is a tighter fit.

Figure 8-6

Figure 8-6a 50 DMA

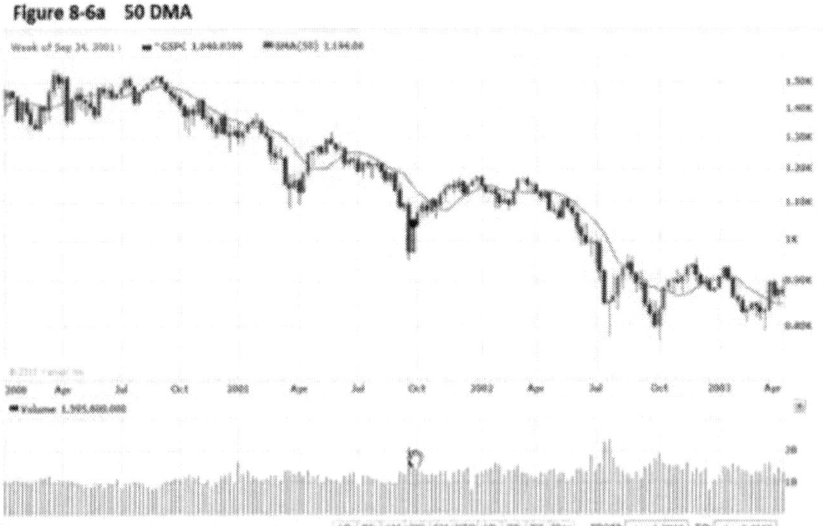

Looking at Figure 8-6a you can see that the 50 DMA tracks closely to the prices and would have had many buy and sell signals, whipsawing back and forth.

You must be especially careful in a sideways market because too many buy and sell signals often lose money during trading ranges. In a sideways market you are better off in cash. The problem is that you do not know which signal will work out beforehand, so you have to take all of them. Otherwise, you do not have a strategy. You should never take some signals and avoid others. That is a path to confusion, loss of discipline, and ultimately, financial ruin.

However, using the 200 DMA alleviates many of the signals and protects your investment capital.

Losing money some of the time is an integral part of any trading system if it is to work. You just need to remember to limit your loss to a maximum 6 to 8% on each trade and if you are stopped out, just sit tight and wait for the next signal before you jump back in.

The Following Chart is the DJIA 5 year with a 200 DMA. This chart was pulled direct from Yahoo. These charts are free – easy – I simply chose 5yr, candlestick style chart for the display and then selected a 200 DMA.

This is a true learning experience. It covers 5 years of investing, and tells us many things.

First: Look on the left side of the chart in December 2005 and early January 2006. Notice that the DJIA crossed the 200 DMA and not only stayed above the moving average, but the moving average was in an upward trend, slanting upward, for almost 2 years. Historically, the 200 DMA serves as 'support' for a stock or index price, and also resistance.

This is clearly shown on the chart from Jan 2006 to Jan 2008 each time the DJIA traded down and touched the 200 DMA it turned and traded higher. Also note that the price penetrated the 200 DMA on 3 occasions during that time and actually traded higher each of those times to close above the average. This shows how powerful the 200 DMA is for acting as a support level for a falling stock or index.

Second: Look at what happened in January 2008. In my book, 'Charting and Technical Analysis', I describe this dark candle as a Bearish Engulfing candle. This one is particularly important because not only does this candle normally signify a change in direction of the market or a particular stock, in this case it also crosses and closes below the 200 day moving average. In the preceding weeks the market had reached an all-time high, and over the past two years each time the market had penetrated the moving average it had still moved back above the average to close.

But in January 2008, this particular week was conclusive evidence that there was possibly a change in the direction of the market taking place. Also note, that is the point that the 200 day moving average changed directions. From this point the moving average turned downward and the market began trading below the average.

Note: Another important thing to remember is that the market or an individual stock will normally not trade too far away from the moving average. This is to say, that if a stock or the market moves too far above or below the moving average it will generally trade lower or higher at some point in time and return to the moving average.

In the following chart the 50 DMA is also included. The 50 DMA has a lot more zigs and zags, but at times can still be helpful in deciding when to be in or out of the market by using Common Sense Investing.

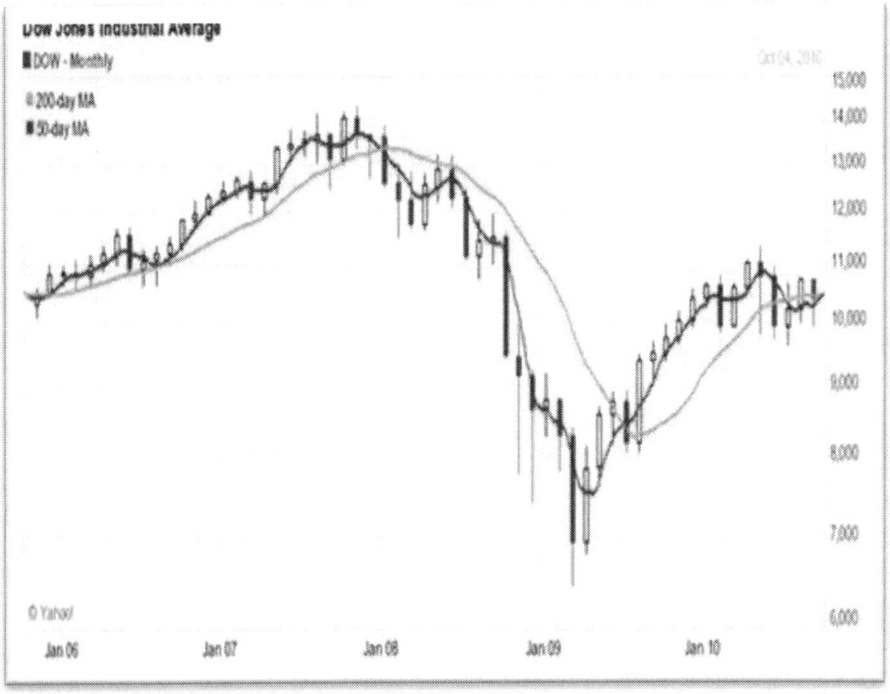

One thing of importance to note is that in January 2008 the 50 DMA crossed the 200 DMA. Consequently, this happened at the same time the bearish engulfing candle formed.

As you look at the chart above, you can see that by using a 50 DMA there were very few times that it would give you a clear signal to buy or sell. At the same time, a five-year chart is not necessarily the best to use making more immediate type decisions. Yet it is a great tool to see the general direction of the market.

The following chart covers only six months.

For the shorter term trader the 50 DMA provides a pretty clear picture as to which direction the market *MAY* take. For instance, as you can see in the above chart every time the DJIA moves away from the 50 DMA within a short period of time it will either move up or down to return to trading close to the average. During this six months time from April 2010 to October 2010 the DJIA crossed the 200 DMA several times. And as I have already pointed out, each time it trades higher or lower away from the 200 DMA, at some point it will again return to the average. You can also see that as the market trades sideways, the 200 DMA levels off and the preceding uptrend becomes a sideways move.

How can this be useful to the individual investor that wants to use Common Sense Investing?

As you can see in April 2010 the DJIA was trading considerably higher than the 200 DMA and is also higher than the 50 DMA. An astute trader would recognize this as it is happening and possibly sell at the top and wait for a correction or pull-back. Also the informed trader or investor would recognize when the stock or index has fallen well below the 200 DMA and possibly look to step in and take advantage of an advance.

Thoughts and Experience

I want to take some time to share some thoughts and experience while looking at this particular chart. As you can see, the 200 DMA smoothes out the action. This is like looking at the market from a bird's eye view. It takes out all of the riffraff, the drama, and the sensationalizing of the "talking heads" on the financial networks. As you probably know if you follow the market closely, every minute of every day there is constantly a new news story of some sort.

Meaning, whatever the market happens to be doing at that particular moment is blamed on, or credited to, some current news event that may or may not even be relevant. Maybe some company released bad news, maybe some other company missed their expected earnings by one penny, or maybe the leader in some third world country woke up in a bad mood. Point is, most everything broadcasted live regarding the market is simply "noise". However, that is one reason to avoid investing in single stocks. It creates too much risk for the individual investor.

Case in point: Looking at the following chart at the period in late 2007 when the market was hitting an all-time-high.

If you will remember, at that time there were numerous 'Talking Heads' on TV spouting all kinds of non-sense about the DJIA would go to 20,000 and the Nasdaq would return to the 5000 level reached in 1999-2000. There were very few that questioned the market at that time or commented that it was overbought, or the housing/mortgage crisis would be a factor. If you watch and listen with an open mind, it is sometimes easy to tell which commentator/prognosticator is invested in 'Long' or 'Short' positions, or maybe is even selling positions and wants the prices to stay high. This is where using simple Common Sense helps rid your thinking of the useless 'Noise'.

Another thing that is important, look at the following chart and note the number of times the 200 DMA is crossed.

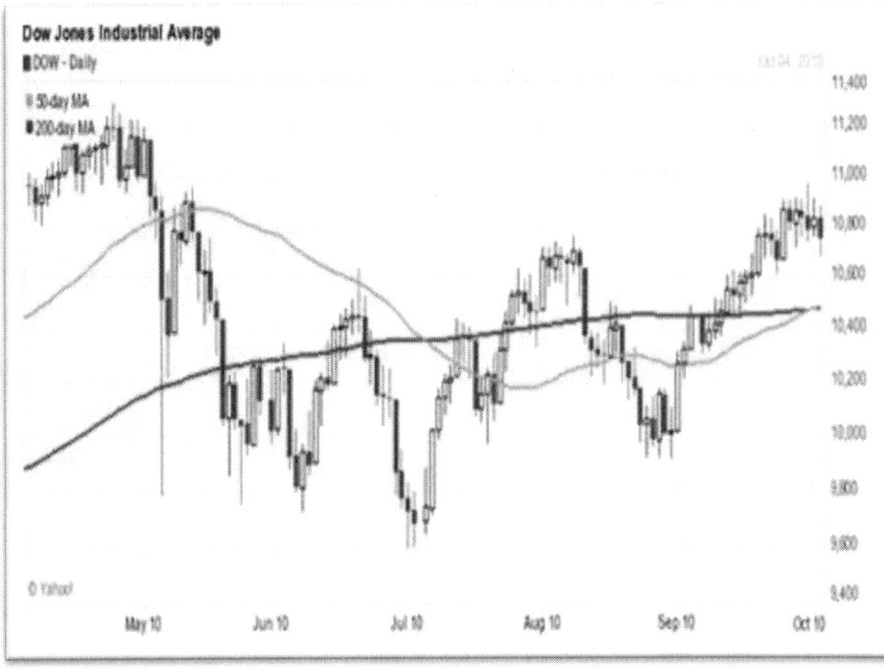

This is a great indicator of a market or stock that is directionless and trading sideways. During this type of action a short-term trader who is able to watch the market constantly might do well. However, this type of action might cause a long term investor to be moving money in and out of the market each time the 200 DMA is crossed. Yet the intelligent investor would recognize this scenario early on and possibly stay in cash until a clear signal is given that it is safe to move back in to the market.

Another Trading Strategy

Another option would be to only buy when the market is significantly lower than the 200 DMA. By waiting for the market to be significantly lower to buy, then your risk is minimized. This strategy has proven successful many times in the past when there was really no clear signal as to when to buy. Maybe the market was trading sideways, or even in an uptrend. Sometimes you need to wait for a pullback to find an entry point.

When buying only on a pullback or correction, you place the odds in your favor that even if there is not much advance in the market, a bounce back up in price will mean you are in positive territory for your position. Stop Losses are absolutely mandatory. See Stop losses covered later in this book.

Common Sense Conclusion

When investing, a little Common Sense can go a long way. For instance, when the market was at or near an all time high, wouldn't any prudent Common Sense Investor be a little skeptical? Sure, regardless of how many times TV personalities and spin doctors claimed that the housing and mortgage crisis would not affect the market like the Dot Com bubble did, a logical thinking Investor would be highly skeptical.

You don't have to watch TV or read the news to know when the economy is in trouble. It affects you and people that you know. You know when gas prices are ridiculously high. You know when homes are being foreclosed. You know when people are losing their jobs or when jobs are plentiful.

It's about using your knowledge to make good decisions and not step into the market when times are bad. Wait until everyone else is giving up, and then look for the bargains.

CHAPTER FOURTEEN

By the Numbers

Now that you know how using the moving averages can help you, let's put some numbers to it and make it real.

The following chart (Figure 8-7) is the **SPY (S&P 500 Index ETF)** for 2000 to 2003 with a 200 DMA.

Look on the left side of the chart during 2000 when the S&P 500 was at its high. When the SPY crossed and closed below the 200 DMA, it was trading at $145.28 per share.

Let's just say you had $150,000 invested at the time. You would have owned 1032 shares of SPY. Since it traded lower and crossed the 200 DMA, you sold your shares on or about September 25th, 2000 and placed your money in a Money Market.

Remember, you are not taking any risks, you are not *Shorting the Market*, you are simply sitting on your $150,000 waiting for an opportunity to re-invest. By the way, there are old-timers that wait for years for the opportunity to buy into the market.

"The time to buy is when there's blood in the streets"
~Baron Rothchild

As you can see by the chart, you would have not re-entered the market until April 2003 since the SPY did not cross back over the 200 DMA but once very briefly. We are not even going to try to calculate and include the interest you would have earned on your money from September 2000 to April 2003. You know you could have probably gotten at least a couple of percentage points of interest that would have added up to several thousand dollars during that time.

In April 2003 when the SPY crossed back over the 200 DMA it was trading at $89.56 per share.
Let's look at a couple of scenarios:

1. Let's say you have a Buddy, and he had held his 1032 original shares and not sold out, now at $89.56 per share he would have a value of $92.425.00 in his account, down 61%.

But instead, you used your Common Sense and sold, so now you are sitting on your $150,000, plus a few dollars interest.

2. Now you can buy 1675 shares of SPY at $89.56 per share.

Of course you might even want to play it safe and only buy half at this point and buy more later, but we'll just act like you wanted to get back 100% invested.

On April 14th, 2003 the SPY closes above the 200 DMA at $89.56 and you buy 1675 shares, you are now re-invested.

The following chart is a continuation of the previous one. The SPY 2003 through 2004 with a 200 DMA.

You have pretty smooth sailing for 15 months, and only touch the 200 DMA one time.
But July 21st, 2004 is a different story. The SPY closed down at 109.58, and below the 200 DMA. It's time to sell.

Now let's look at our scenarios, and how they are fairing.

1. Remember that 1032 shares your Buddy held on to? His account value would be $113,086.00. Almost 4 years later, and still down significantly.

2. But instead, you are selling 1675 shares at $109.58 for a total of $183,546.00.

Obviously you see the difference. By holding on, as we discussed earlier in the book, it can take many years to get back to break-even. And in this case, Almost 4 years have passed and still, your buddy who is holding his shares is not even close.

Now it gets interesting. When you look at the continuing chart from July to November 2004, the SPY crosses back and forth across the 200 DMA several times.

After selling your shares, from July to November 2004 the SPY crossed the 200 DMA 5 times. However, by following your investing strategy you would have never lost more than about $4.00 per share, and no more than 2 times. And as I mentioned earlier, when you suspect a sideways market, sometimes the best technique is to either wait for a pullback and buy when the stock or index is significantly lower than the average.

This usually works well in an up-trending market because most often the index or stock will trade back to the moving average after a pull-back or correction.

But remember, if the moving average is sloping downward, this is not a feasible strategy.

There are other techniques described in my book, *'Charting and Technical Analysis'* that teach you to identify the chart patterns and candlesticks on the chart with regard to pin-pointing a top or bottom in the price movements.

The above chart shows that the SPY crossed over the 200 DMA on October 30th, 2004 and you would have bought again at $113.22, investing about $183,000 buying 1590 shares of SPY.

Let's continue follow our investing plan.

With a couple of 'hick-ups' along the way, you are invested until November 12, 2007. The SPY closes below the 200 DMA, and it's time to sell again.

Looking at our continuing scenario.

1. Your Buddy, still holding the original 1032 shares, would now be back to break even with an account valued at $150,455.00. It only took 7 ½ years to get back to Break-even status.
2. By selling your 1590 shares of Spy at $145.79, you now have an account balance of $231,806.00. Once again, you place your money in a Money Market to draw interest until another buying opportunity presents itself.

As we continue, our next chart continues from the time of your sale to your next buy point.

The Bear Market of 2008-09 was insufferable for the Buy and Hold crowd. But on June 1st, 2009, 19 months after your last sale, the SPY crosses the 200 DMA once more at $94.77 per share.

This is what our scenarios look like at this point.

1. Your Buddy with his original 1032 shares, now for almost 10 years, has an account value of $97,802.00. Even though this amount is UP from the low in March 2009 of $68.11 per share, and a total value of $70,289.00, it is still a far cry from the $150,000 where it started nearly 10 years ago.
2. But the intelligent Common Sense Investor is ready to re-invest at $94.77 per share. And with the $231,806.00 that has been safely drawing interest you can buy about 2,437 shares.

Let's take a quick look at one more transaction, since your first sale on September 25th, 2000, our next chart brings us to 10 years of investing.

As you can see, after your last purchase at $94.77, there were a couple of small bumps, but never had a confirming close under the 200 DMA. Then the SPY advanced, staying above the moving average for close to a year. Then in May, 2010, it was time to sell once again. 2437 shares were sold at $109.11 for a total of $265,901.00.

In checking on your buddy who held his original 1032 shares of SPY, his account value is now $112,601.00.

Sure, in looking at the above chart, you could have been greedy and sold at $120.00 or more just a few days earlier. You could have even shorted the SPY at times and earned far more than the interest earned in the Money market. But that would require more trades, more risk, and being more active as an Investor. But this example is on the conservative side.

I would just remind you to refer back to the 'REASONS' the Financial Advisors and Investment Firms want you to Buy-and-Hold. Then use your Common Sense to decide what is best for you and your financial future.

This Common Sense Investing Strategy using the 200 DMA is about as simple as it gets. It doesn't require constantly watching the market, listening to 'Talking Heads', or any emotion whatsoever when the market is up a few dollars today or down a few cents tomorrow.

Each decision to buy or sell is made without emotion and simply followed religiously. And above all, it preserves your capital and allows you to take advantage of the bear markets and buy at or near the bottom and sell at or near the top.

Conclusion

There are many ways to use the moving-averages in investing. Some Investors and Traders even use the 200 DMA and a 50 DMA as a dual moving average. In doing so, the buy and sell signals are given when the 50 DMA crosses the 200 DMA. Other variations are used as well, but these types of strategies require more trades and being a much more active 'Trader', instead of an 'Investor'.

But for the Common Sense Investor who does not wish to stress and fret over the daily gyrations in the market, the 200 DMA just makes good Common Sense.

CHAPTER FIFTEEN

Bond Investing

Not all investments are good, and some good investments are bad for some investors. It can be devastating for the average investor when they are sold an investment, a Mutual Fund, or even Bonds, only to watch the value decrease after the purchase.

Remember this: When investing, "Timing" is everything.

During the past 25 years of trading and investing I have seen it happen countless times. As the stock market advances, the wrong investments continue to be sold to the unknowing investor. And then as the market declines, the same thing happens, individuals being sold the wrong investments again at the wrong time.

For instance, in 1999-2000 and again in 2007 as the market approached an all-time high, Financial Advisors continued to sell Mutual Funds and other investments that would certainly drop in value during *ANY* market correction, and would especially take a major hit when (not if) a bear market ensued.

Then during the bear market, the interest rates drop to their lowest point in years and the salespeople start selling Bonds and fixed income investments because the public is too scared to buy Stock Funds. This is once again *ABSOLUTELY* the wrong time to invest in Bonds.

This reoccurring scenario continually places the individual investor on the wrong side of the market on every investment they make. With a rising market and a good economy selling an investment in a Mutual Fund to John Q. Public is an easy sale. Everyone wants on the 'Band Wagon'. Charts and graphs can be presented showing how well a particular investment might be doing. And the unknowing, and unsuspecting investor is once again taken for a ride, and a cleaning. Problem is, everyone is a genius during the good times, and every Salesperson can present compelling information to look as though the average investor will make money hand over fist. But the sales become much more difficult during a declining market, and it never fails, during bad economic times the sales person will sell ***whatever*** they can regardless whether it is good or bad for the investor.

During every bad economic time, recession, or Bear market, one of the classic investments sold are Bonds. And why not? During bad times the investing public sees their portfolio destroyed by a declining market, they are scared, disappointed, dissatisfied, and at the same time, they know they need investment income, they just don't know what to do about it. So they flee to the safety of a fixed income investment where they know exactly what return they will receive.

Are Bonds a good investment? Sure, they can be, but it depends upon what the particular individual investor needs. In other words, selling a 30 year bond to a 70 year old widow simply because the bond pays 1% or 2% more than her CD at the bank, is probably not a good idea. She may need access to her money sometime before her 100th birthday. Or an individual investor buying a bond while interest rates are at 1% or 2% because of their safety may not be a very good idea either. But believe it or not, this happens often.

When stock prices are down and the value of mutual funds have been decimated, investors are scared of further declines, and bonds become a salable item for Financial Advisors. The investor flees to safety and unknowingly is "Set-Up" for another major hit on their investment account.

Why is this not a good time to buy bonds?

Let's first look at how Bond Pricing actually works.

Bond prices and interest rates are on an inverted scale. As interest rates decline, bond prices go up. At first glance, the inverse relationship between interest rates and bond prices seems somewhat illogical, but upon closer examination, it makes sense. An easy way to grasp why bond prices move opposite to interest rates is to consider zero-coupon bonds. These bonds don't pay interest payments to the bond holders on a scheduled basis. The bond holder receives their interest, or profit, from the difference between the purchase price they paid for the bond and the par value the bond will pay the holder at maturity.

For instance, if a zero-coupon bond is trading at $950 and has a par value of $1,000 (paid at maturity in one year), the bond's rate of return at the present time is approximately 5.26% ((1000-950) / 950 = 5.26%).

For a person to pay $950 for this bond, he or she must be happy with receiving a 5.26% return. But his or her satisfaction with this return depends on what else is happening in the bond market. Bond investors, like all investors, typically try to get the best return possible. If current interest rates were to rise, giving newly issued bonds a yield of 10%, then the zero-coupon bond yielding 5.26% would not only be less attractive, it wouldn't be in demand at all. Who wants a 5.26% yield when they can get 10%? To attract demand, the price of the pre-existing zero-coupon bond would have to decrease enough to match the same return yielded by prevailing interest rates. In this instance, the bond's price would drop from $950 (which gives a 5.26% yield) to $909 (which gives a 10% yield).

Now that we have an idea of how a bond's price moves in relation to interest-rate changes, it's easy to see why a bond's price would increase if prevailing interest rates were to drop. If rates dropped to 3%, our zero-coupon bond - with its yield of 5.26% - would suddenly look very attractive. More people would buy the bond, which would push the price up until the bond's yield matched the prevailing 3% rate. In this instance, the price of the bond would increase to approximately $970. This would be a $20 profit for the bond holder that originally paid $950, if it were sold while the interest rates were low.

Now, with bond pricing and their relationship to interest rates in mind, what does Common Sense tell you about purchasing bonds?

The economy is cyclical. During downturns in the economy, declines in the stock market, and recessionary times, supply and demand continue to work in the markets. To ease the strain on the economy and diminish the toll that either a recession, or an impending recession might have on the economy, the Federal Reserve begins dropping the discount rate charged to banks. This is normally done in small increments of 25 basis points at a time, although there have been more severe cases when there was a cut of 50 or 75 basis points after the Federal Reserve's scheduled meeting.

If you remember, the Federal Reserve increased interest rates prior to the 2000-02 Bear market. The Federal Reserve chairman, Alan Greenspan made many comments regarding the 'Irrational Exuberance' of the Dot Com craze. So with the concern that companies with no real income were experiencing astronomical prices for their stock, rates were raised to tighten the money supply.
But eventually, the rates were once again cut to help end the Bear market and stabilize the economy.

During hard times, as these discount rates are cut, interest rates decline making money more accessible in order to stimulate the economy, thereby easing the pain of an economic downturn.

So, to buy bonds when the economy is bad and the interest rates are low is a double whammy for the investor. Remember, bond prices and interest rates move on an inverted scale. Meaning, as interest rates decline, bond prices increase. And as interest rates increase, bond prices fall. Therefore, when interest rates are at their lowest, the average investor will likely pay a premium for the bond.
Conversely, as interest rates begin to move higher, the bond prices will move down.

So in essence, by listening to a Financial Advisor or TV personality that is a market Guru 'wannabe', the average investor takes a hit two times:

1. They are invested in a fund purchased during a rising market that may, or may not ever return to the value of their purchase price. Their Fund investments decline with the market and - that is their first hit.
2. They are sold bonds while interest rates are low and the market is down which sets them up for their - next hit.

As the economy improves the interest rates will begin to rise once again. As this happens, the bond prices will drop. The unknowing investor is then either stuck with a fixed income Bond paying only a few percentage points in income for 10, 20, or maybe 30 years, and the only way to get out of this investment and re-invest in something more attractive, is to take the loss. Another loss.

As I mentioned earlier, "**Timing is Everything**".

When interest rates are low and the market is down is ***NOT*** the time to be buying bonds. Bonds should normally be purchased while interest rates are high and can then be sold for a profit when interest rates fall. Remember? As interest rates fall, the price (value) of your bond increases.

The following charts depict exactly the inverse relationship between bond prices, interest rates, and stock prices.
First, look at January to October 2008 as the Federal Reserve made 5 rate cuts during the 2007 - 2009 Bear Market. Then look at the Bond Price chart how the prices were on a steady increase during this time.

DATE	DISCOUNT RATE			FEDERAL FUNDS RATE	
	CHANGE	NEW LEVEL* PRIMARY[1]	NEW LEVEL* SECONDARY[2]	CHANGE	NEW LEVEL
2008					
Dec 16	-.75	0.50	1.00	-1 to -.75	0.00 - 0.25
Oct 29	-.50	1.25	1.75	-.50	1.00
Oct 8	-.50	1.75	2.25	-.50	1.50
Apr 30	-.25	2.25	2.75	-.25	2.00
Mar 18	-.75	2.50	3.00	-.75	2.25
Mar 16	-.25	3.25	3.75		
Jan 30	-.50	3.50	4.00	-.50	3.00
Jan 22	-.75	4.00	4.50	-.75	3.50

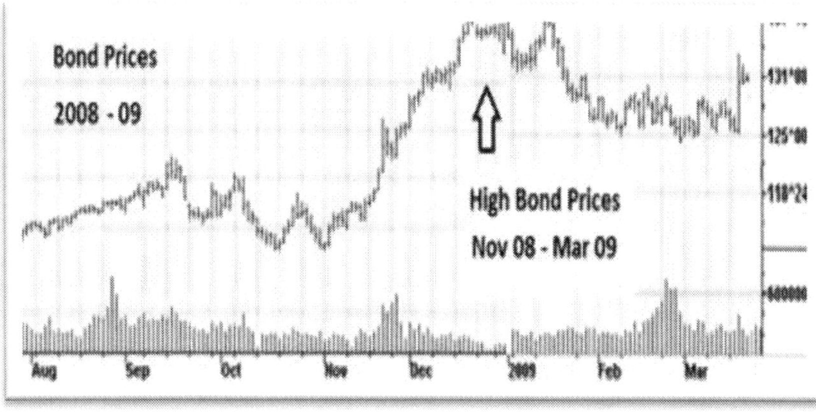

Note the 2 large rate cuts (50 basis points each) in October 2008 and what happened to the Bond prices immediately after the cut on October 29th.

As you can see, Bond prices reached their highest point with the December 2008 rate cut of 75 basis points.

Now, look at what was happening in the stock market at that same exact time.

Clearly, during the time when the market was at its lowest point, the Federal Reserve was attempting to stimulate the economy by cutting rates, the stock prices were down, the interest rates were down, and the Bond prices were UP.

From a realistic perspective, this is what happens to the individual investor. As the market declines, worry, discouragement, and disappointment ensues, and then when a broker or Financial Advisor presents the investor with a Bond as an investment that is paying more than the CD rates, they buy it.
What can you, as the Common Sense Investor do with this knowledge? Where can you 'Park' your money after you sell your other investments?

As an Investing strategy, Bonds are no different than stocks. Remember, "Buy Low – Sell High".

Think about it. While interest rates are up and the economy is churning along, the Bond yields are up but Bond Prices are down. As was the case in 2007, remember the sale you made at the top of the market? See the following chart.

When you made the above sale in November 2007, the economy was yet to go into recession and the stock market was near an all- time-high. What a great time to buy some Bonds as the Bear market takes hold, recession begins, interest rates are cut, the stock market declines, and you watch the price of those bonds increase.

Yes, you would be buying a 'Fixed income' investment, but remember, you can sell those bonds for a profit or a loss at any time depending on the current prices. You are essentially 'Parking' your money in a safe place, and when the prices increase; you are obviously going to receive a better return on your money than a Money Market account.

Common Sense Conclusion

As I just mentioned, buying Bonds while interest rates are high when you exited the market would have been a great investment. Remember, the average length of a Bear Market is more than 17 months. And by holding a Bond that is paying higher interest, not only do you profit from receiving the higher rate of return, when interest rates fall, you can capitalize by selling the bond for a profit. This is a safe way to make money 'on your money' while it is parked.

It is not uncommon to find bonds paying 8 to 10% during bad economic periods. Even Municipal Bonds, which rate closely to government bonds in safety, may pay 7%, and most all municipal bonds are tax free.

Yet, as it always happens, when the market is down, interest rates are down, and the economy looks bleak, uninformed investors will pay a premium for a higher interest bond because they are scared of the stock market after taking a beating during the decline.

CHAPTER SIXTEEN

Shorting the Market

'Going Short' has been mentioned periodically throughout the book. What does that mean?

Shorting the Market, Index, or an individual stock means that you actually sell shares of that stock or ETF without owning any. If you believe that a stock or market index is overvalued, overbought, and likely to drop, you could sell shares without actually owning any yet and that would be "shorting" the stock or the index. Then you would later buy back shares to close your position. If the stock has dropped as anticipated so that you can buy it at a lower price, you've made money.

It sounds complicated and possibly confusing, but it really is not. It is the opposite of Buying Low and Selling High. When Shorting, it is the reverse, your objective is to Sell High and Buy Low. To accomplish this, you are in essence borrowing the shares from your Broker to sell while the price is high, then when the price of the shares fall as you expect, you buy the shares back at the lower price to replace the shares that you borrowed from your Broker. Since you sold *High* and re-purchased *Low*, then your profit is the difference in price between the sale and purchase.

An example:

If you believe the stock price of ABC is grossly overvalued and is going to crash sometime soon. You sell Short 100 shares of ABC at the current market price for $50. (100 shares x $50 per share = $5000)

The following week, the price of ABC stock falls to $20 per share. You call your broker and buy 100 shares of ABC stock, at the new price of $20 per share to close your Short position. You pay him the $2000 (100 shares x $20 per share = $2000).

Do you see what happened? You borrowed the shares of ABC, sold them for $5000. The following week, when ABC fell to $20 per share, you repurchased those 100 shares for $2000. Your profit is the difference of $3000.

Let's look at another real life example.

The following chart is one used earlier of the S&P 500 (SPY).

Figure 8-7

When you sold your shares of SPY earlier would have been a good time to take a small Short position by selling SPY short. Just to be safe, you could have waited a week or two after selling out at $145.28 and just watched to see if SPY would turn and move back above the moving average.

Remember? The Moving Average normally is 'Support' while the stock or index is above it, but also works as 'Resistance' when the stock or index is below it.

The above chart is a classic case. The SPY fell below the 200 DMA and a few days later tried to rally back above it but it was unable to do so. When it could not close above the 200 DMA was a perfect time to sell it 'Short'.

There are alternatives in this type of trade.

1. You can simply move your Stop Loss down to protect your profit, always giving it some 'breathing room'. If you are 'Stopped out', then wait for it to trade back close to the 200 DMA and sell it Short again.

2. Keep your Stop Loss in a profitable position but high enough you don't get Stopped Out, then ride it down.

What would have happened if you had only Shorted the Spy using half your investment capital, played it safe and kept your Stop Loss in a profitable position and rode it down?

To keep it simple, let's just say you are the conservative type and only sold 500 shares Short at $140 per share. That would be using $70,000 of your investment capital for a short position.

Even if you waited till it was time to buy again when the SPY crossed back over the 200 DMA, you would have closed out your Short position by buying back the 500 shares at about $90 per share.

Gain = $25,000, about a 35% return on your investment.

I'll let you use your Common Sense to determine what you would really have done in that situation. But Shorting can be profitable, especially when done correctly.

No, I'm not suggesting you dump all of your investments in long positions and just start shorting stocks. What I am saying is use your Common Sense, look at it realistically and logically.

Realistically, what are the chances of finding the next big winner? Remember the statistics from earlier?

- 64% of stocks underperformed the Russell 3000 from 1983 - 2006, dividends included.
- 39% of stocks had a negative lifetime total return. **Two out of every five stocks lose money**.
- 19% of stocks lost at least 75% of their value. **Almost one stock out of every five is a really bad investment**.

How hard is it to find a stock that will advance 20% per year? Of the 5,869 stocks on major U.S. exchanges, only 248, or about 4% of them, had compounded annual returns of 20% or more over the 10 year period from 2000 - 2010.

So you shouldn't spend so much of your time looking for big winners. Instead, put the odds in your favor and focus on the 64% of stocks that stink. You may even come across some of the really ugly ones -- the one out of five stocks that will go on to lose 75% of their value. Remember, the odds of finding a big loser are almost *five times* better than the odds of finding a big winner!

Risk of Shorting

Many fear being 'Short' because of the risk involved. And it is true, Shorting does involve more risk than being *Long*, or buying. For example, if you buy 100 shares of a $20 stock and it goes to $0, you have lost your entire investment of $2,000, but you knew your maximum risk was $2,000 when you purchased, right? However, if you short a $20 stock and suddenly some news comes out that shoots the stock price up to, say $50, your loss is now $3,000 and can keep rising.

That's what makes shorting stocks the riskier investment and why many don't like to do it. They see the risk as 'unlimited'. Which in theory, it is unlimited risk. But that is what Stop Losses are for. You use a Stop Loss in a Short position for the same reason you use one in a long position. You don't want to lose ALL your money if your investment falls to $0.00, nor do you want to lose ALL your money if you are Short and the price goes to the 'Infinite.' So you use a Stop Loss to prevent either scenario.

However, being 'Short' a stock or an index can be used as a tool to protect your investments. There are several alternatives in doing this.

1. Set aside a chunk of your portfolio for shorts. That will act as a useful hedge against your favorite long positions and give your portfolio a critical ballast during tough times in the market. Just imagine if 20% of your portfolio would have been short going into the 2002 or 2008 market crash. Imagine how much better you could have done.

2. When you sell your investments at a market top, then allocate a percentage to a short position while placing the rest of your money in a cash position.

3. During a Bear Market, Short only in small increments. For instance, 15 to 20% of your investment capital in a Short position at a time, and move your Stop Loss down as your positions become more profitable. Always remember, The Stop Loss protects your Investment – *AND* – your profit.

It really is not that complicated. It only takes Common Sense and using the available tools to capitalize on the opportunities as they present themselves.

Shorting can also be accomplished through Funds that specialize in short positions. Since the Market, and the price of individual stocks always fall much faster than they rise, shorting can be very profitable.

Common Sense Conclusion

Shorting is a very valuable tool. Realizing that stock prices and the market in general always falls faster than it rises, it is just Common Sense to take advantage of that opportunity. Always remember to protect your Investment, first and foremost, with a Stop Loss. Then you know going in what your maximum loss might be whether you are Long or Short. That is the Key!

CHAPTER SEVENTEEN

Options Strategy

For some, the thought of following the market and buying and selling a few times a year might be too much to deal with. Some even fear that they will be hit with Capital Gains tax for selling and buying, even though this was covered earlier with regard to being taxed on the Capital gains of a Mutual Fund when the Fund declares the gain or loss, the fear of taxes still hamper some investors.

In 2007 I mentioned to a friend of mine that he should take steps to protect his retirement since I suspected another Bear Market was inevitable. He assured me that he was well diversified and did not want to be hit with taxes for selling any of his holdings. Even though this is the attitude of many investors, the realization they should have done something different always hits when the Bear Market ensues.

Hopefully, by learning what can happen by 'Holding' an investment, one would rather pay taxes on money that you have, instead of not paying taxes because you have no money.

Regardless, there is another way, Options.

Options can be used as a protection strategy for your investments. Options can also be used to 'Short' a stock or an ETF.

Many simply do not understand Options, and they think of them as risky, lottery tickets, or make some other derogatory reference to the use of options.

In case you do not understand Options, let me explain them in their simplest form.

There are two basic **types** of options: **Calls and Puts**.

Let's make sure you understand the concepts of long and short calls and puts by using a pizza coupon and car insurance analogy. If you are in possession of a pizza coupon, you have an 'Option.' You are "long" the coupon and have the right, but not the obligation, to buy one pizza for a fixed price over a given time period. In the real world, you do not buy pizza coupons; they are handed out for free. But that doesn't put an end to our analogy because the basic idea is still the same. This coupon would be the same as if you had purchased a Call Option on a Stock or Index Fund.

Since you are holding the coupon, that means you possess the right to use it, and that's the role of the Long position in an Option. The pizza storeowner would be "Short" the coupon and has an *obligation* to sell you the pizza for the price listed on the coupon, if you choose to use your coupon. In the same scenario, whoever sold you the Call Option has the obligation to sell you the Stock at the price listed on the Option until the Option expires.

You have the right; he has the obligation.

If you buy an auto insurance policy you are "Long" the policy and have the right to "Put" your car back to the insurance company. The insurance company is "Short" the policy; it receives money in exchange for the potential obligation of having to buy your car from you. Whether you make a claim or not, the insurance company keeps your premium just as the seller of an Option, and just as you would if you Sold an Option.

That's the Insurance Company's compensation for accepting the risk, the premium.

In the real world of car insurance, you cannot just force the Insurance Company to buy the car back for any reason. There are certain conditions that must be met; for example, the car must be damaged or stolen. You can't just obligate the insurance company because you don't like your car anymore or because it has depreciated in value.

However, in the real world of Put options, you *CAN* sell your stock at a fixed price for *any* reason while your Put Option is still in effect. There are no restrictions. Of course, you wouldn't want to do that if the fixed price you'd receive is less than the current market price. The main point is that if you are long, or Buy, a Put Option, you call the shots. You have the rights. You have the "option" to decide. You have the right to sell your stock for that fixed price at any time during the time your "policy" (Option Contract) is in effect.

Most option contracts are opened and closed in the open market without a single share of stock ever changing hands. Even though you're allowed to purchase or sell stock with your options, most people never do. Instead, they just buy and sell the contracts in the open market amongst other traders.

Understanding a Put Option

How can this possibly be of value to protecting your Investments?

Let's look at a scenario.

Remember, you do not need to own the shares of the stock or index fund (SPY, QQQQ, or DIA) to buy a Put Option. But if you owned shares of SPY and feared the market was about to head lower, by purchasing a Put Option, you have the right to sell your shares for the amount (strike price) of your Option Contract, the specified price, for a designated period of time. So, in essence, you are purchasing a Put Option at a price near the current market value of your shares for a period of time, and this "insurance" only costs you the amount of the Option. And since Options trade for a fraction of the price of the underlying stock or ETF, then you are basically "buying insurance."

Let's look at the Option prices for a stock to get an example.

The following Table is the Option Chain on SPY. As you can see, at the top, SPY is currently selling at $118.94 per share. Directly to the right of the current market price you'll see the current date is October 21st. Then right below that, you see the column for 'Calls' and another column for 'Puts'. The top series of columns are for the Options that expire in November, and the bottom series is for Options that expire in December. You will notice different prices for longer periods of time. Meaning, Options that expire in November are less than those expiring in December. Shorter time, less money.

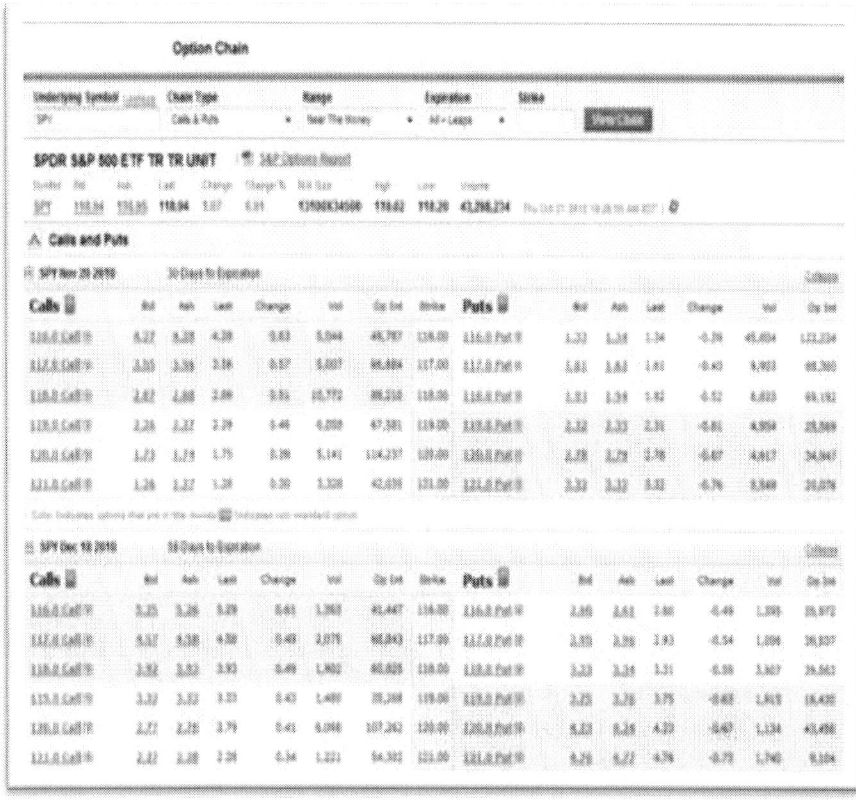

Now, for example, if you owned 100 shares of SPY as an investment and feared the market was headed down and the value in your investment account could fall, you could buy a Put Option to protect your investment account. For instance, if you buy a 116.00 Put Option at the 'Ask price' for $1.34, then you would have the right to sell 100 shares of SPY at $116.00 per share at any time from the day of purchase (October 21st) until the 3rd Friday of November. Thirty days to be exact.

Remember, each Option contract is for 100 shares of stock, so you must multiply the Ask price of $1.34 X 100 = $134.00.

So realistically, if you owned 100 shares of SPY and it is currently selling at $118.94 per share, your investment is actually worth $11,894.00. And for $134.00 you can guarantee that your investment will not fall below $116.00 per share for thirty days. If the stock price falls, then you have the Option to sell it for $116.00 per share even if the stock price fell to $0.00. That is 'Insurance,' plain and simple.

Does this mean you just threw away $134.00? No. Your Option Contract will change in value throughout the day, every day, as the price of the underlying stock fluctuates. It may decrease in value the closer it gets to expiration, but it still has value depending on the current selling price of the underlying stock. For instance, if the stock price of SPY increases, then your Put Option value will obviously decrease since the market price is higher than the price on your Option, selling at $116.00 when the current market price is higher is not a good deal, obviously. But if the stock price falls in value, then your Put Option value will increase because it then has value. And obviously, the more the stock price declines, the more valuable your Option would become.

If the stock price fell $10.00 per share that does not mean you would have to sell your stock. Instead, you could simply sell your Option prior to its expiration for the profit which would offset the decline in the stock price, thus protecting the 'bottom line' in your investment account.

Also note that since the price of the Option is based on the current price of the underlying stock, you have several alternatives.

For instance: If a week or two passes and the stock price has not fallen, your Option may have decreased in value to let's say, maybe $95.00. At that point you could continue to hold that Option, or you could sell it for a small loss and purchase another Put Option for a longer period of time, thus, giving you more time to be protected from a potential decline in your investment.

Selling Call Options

Income Source and Protection

Selling Call Options on Stock that you own is what is referred to as 'Selling Covered Calls.' This is a source of income. This is like the Pizza Store. In our analogy, if the 'Pizza Dude' sold Coupons for their pizza, then he would be obligated to honor those coupons at the price listed on the coupon if you wanted a pizza at that price. This technique produces income from your investment while you are holding the investment waiting for it to increase in value. Or it can be used as a Bearish approach to protecting the value of your account balance.

Let me explain. If you fear a decline in the market, as we just learned, you could buy Put Options to protect the value of your account, continue to hold your stock, and make money on the Options as the price declines, thereby offsetting what would have otherwise been a decline in your account balance.

However, there is another way to accomplish this, and can also easily be used to generate income while the stock is not advancing in price, or maybe you feel it may decline. Selling Covered Calls. This technique can be used at any time as an income generator. Since you already own the stock, buying a Put Option is an expense. However, Selling a Call Option is INCOME!

The difference is this: If you buy a Put Option, the price of the underlying stock must decline in order for you to make money on your Option. Otherwise, the price of the Option is an expense and simply insurance for your account balance. But selling a Covered Call Option is income to your account. When you sell a Covered Call, even if the price of the stock continues to trade sideways and does not decline, you keep the premium you collected for the option, thereby making money.

When looking at it from a Bearish perspective, it would be like the Pizza Store selling coupons that were good for 30 days for 1 large pepperoni pizza for $10.00. If the Pizza Store sold the coupons for $2.00 each, then the Pizza Dude would make money whether anyone ever used (exercised) a coupon or not. If the price of pizzas declined and could be purchased anywhere for $8.00 each, then the coupons would be worthless, right? Exactly, but the Pizza Dude still keeps the money from the sale of the coupons.

Let's look at how you would use this technique in a sideways or declining market.

Displayed below is the same table of Option Contracts for SPY. Look at the Call Option 'Bid Prices' for November.

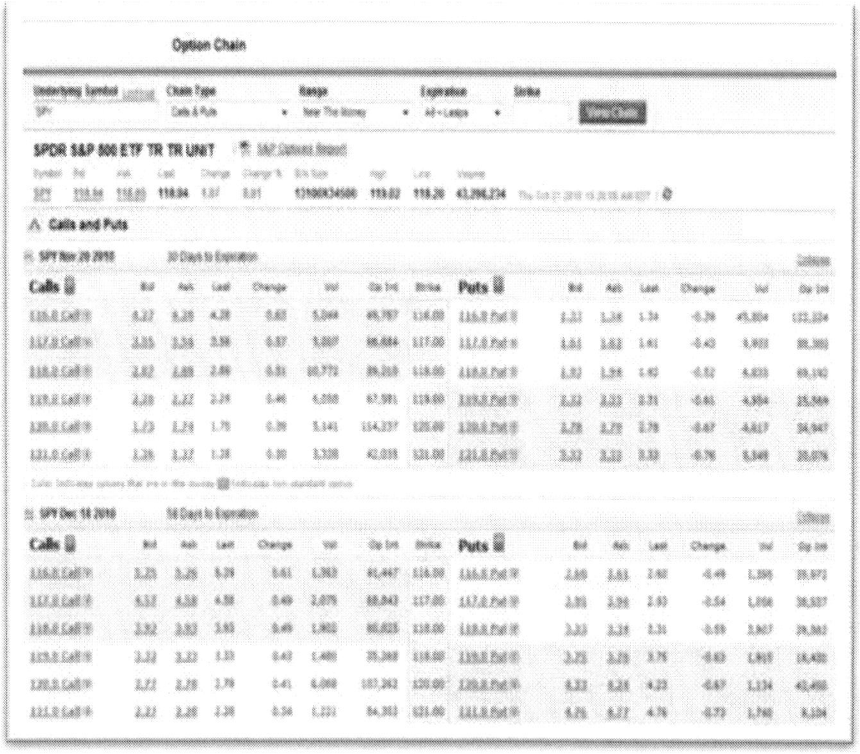

For instance, let's say you owned 500 shares of SPY and maybe had purchased it at a lower price, around $94.00 per share as you did with one of the purchases earlier. Also note that the current market price of SPY is $118.94 shown on the table just above the call options prices. Now look at the Call Option 'Bid Price' for the **November 119.00 Call of 2.26.** Remember, Option price of $2.26 X 100 = $226.00. Also remember, you own 500 shares, so you can sell 5 Covered Call option contracts which would equal $1130.00.

Yes, this means you would be selling a Covered Call Option giving someone the right to buy your 500 shares of SPY stock for $119.00 per share. You would receive $1130.00 in your account as the 'premium' for these contracts. Remember, the current price of SPY is $118.94. So you sold the Covered Call Options just above the current price of the stock.

Understandably, no one is going to exercise the Option and buy your stock unless the stock price increases above $118.94.

Therefore, you are thinking that either the market is trading sideways, or that SPY's stock price is ***not*** going to increase before the Option expires, and the Option will expire in 30 days, worthless. That way you keep the $1130.00 premium and sell another 5 Option contracts next month doing the same thing again.

What is the worst case scenario?

The worst possible thing that could happen is the price of SPY Stock increases and the Option is 'called' (exercised), and you are forced to sell the stock. So what?

Look at it this way. The buyer of the Option paid $1134.00 as a premium for the "right" to purchase the 500 shares of stock at $119.00. That means that since the buyer already paid $2.26 per share for the 'right' to buy, then the stock price would have to be above $121.26 (119.00 + 2.26 = 121.26) in order for the buyer to break even. Therefore, most likely, this buyer would not 'Call' the option and make you sell unless the price was far enough above $121.26 to be a profitable transaction.

If, and that is a big 'If,' the stock price increased enough for the Option to be exercised within the next 30 days, then you would be selling your stock for $121.26 per share. The Option price of $119.00 + $2.26 per share collected on the Option premium. If this happened, that would mean that the price of SPY stock advanced more than $2.32 per share in a month. Can it happen? Sure, but not likely if the market is weak at the time and you are expecting it to fall. If it does, then you made a profit and can buy the stock back during a pullback or market correction.

Let's say for instance the price did increase and you did not want to sell your stock. Another alternative would be to simply buy back the option, cancelling out the sale you made.

By selling out-of-the-money Call options like we just discussed, you can produce income from your investments during any kind of market. During a declining Bear market, selling Call Options generates income, or you can buy Put Options that will increase in value as the stock prices decline also adding income to your account. Conversely, during an advancing Bull Market, selling Call Options for prices higher than the current stock price generates income as well.

Option Spread

Want a Guarantee to NOT Lose Money?

Are you scared? Are you afraid you're wrong in thinking the market will decline, and instead of trading sideways or declining it will go up and you'll lose your 500 shares of SPY?

Don't worry; you can buy 'Insurance' EVEN on your Option! The Option Spread.

Traders who deal in Options use many different types of Option 'Spreads.' There are Butterfly Spreads, Debit Spreads, Credit Spreads, Straddles, and many other variations.

But for the individual investor, the investor who fears the market might advance when least expected and his Covered Call Option might get 'called,' the most basic type of 'Spread' to protect your stock is the Bear Call Spread. This is actually a Credit Spread that will generate income with only a small risk, and protect your account balance at the same time. The strategy is to 'Sell a Call' and 'Buy a Call' **at the same time**. That sounds ridiculous doesn't it?

Well, it's not ridiculous, and here is how it works. Let's look at our Option Chain for SPY again.

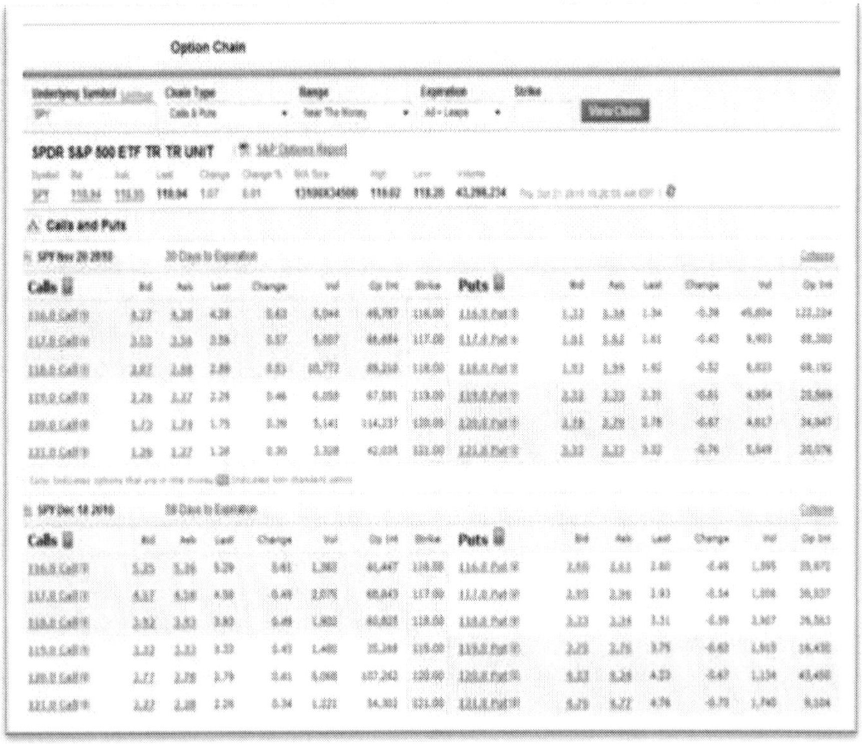

Remember, you were selling 5 Covered Call Options for your 500 shares of SPY at $119.00 for 2.26. Now look at the Option Chain again just below the 2.26 price for the 119.00 Call options.

The 121.00 Call Options are 1.26, and both the 1.19 and the 1.21 Call Options expire at the exact same time, on the same day.

To cover your sale of Cover Calls, simply buy 5 of the 121.00 Options for 1.26. That's right. You sold 5 Contracts at 2.26 and bought 5 Contracts at 1.26.

Now let's look at the numbers.

$1134.00 Income from the sale of your 5 Covered Calls at 2.26.

$630.00 Paid to buy 5 Calls at 121.00.

$504.00 Net income in your account.

Now then, what can happen? What are the scenarios?

1. The price of SPY trades sideways for the next 30 days fluctuating very little, and both the 119.00 and the 121.00 Option Contracts expire worthless.

   You made $504 in 30 days.

2. The price of SPY declines. It doesn't matter how much, because any decline will cause both the 119.00 and the 121.00 Call Options to expire worthless.

   You still made $504.00

3. The price of Spy rallies and advances above both option prices, let's say to $126.00 per share, although it doesn't matter how high it goes, because you bought an Option for the 'right' to purchase SPY at $121.00.

   In this scenario, your maximum loss is always the difference in the strike price of the options, less the net income received from the sale and purchase. Therefore, there is $2.00 difference in the strike prices (121.00 – 119.00) for 5 contracts equaling $1000 less the $504 net premium you received.

   Total Maximum Loss is $496.00

Obviously, in this scenario the investor is doubtful the price would increase, therefore would be comfortable in making the money from collecting the premium from the sale of the options.

However, even in the worst case scenario, where the price of SPY advanced from $118.94 to $126.00 per share causing a loss of $496.00, what is the ***REAL*** bottom line?

You still own your 500 shares, and would have realized a $7.00 per share gain in the stock price equal to $3,500.00.

So in reality, there really is no worst-case scenario. If the price of SPY remains the same or declines, you made money on the options, and if SPY advances, you made money on the stock and lost a fraction on the options. Thus, you made money either way.

No Loss or Limited Loss Strategy

Another advantage to the above strategy is to limit even the loss of the option contracts in the event the stock is advancing in price. This way, you make money on the stock that is advancing, and you do not lose money, or you at least limit the amount you lose on the Option contracts.

Remember, as the price of the stock advances, the option contracts are becoming more valuable as the stock price increases.

In this scenario, as the price of SPY increases, the individual that purchased the 5 contracts from you would see an increase in value of the call options he is now holding. But you are also holding 5 contracts that will also increase in value at the same time.

This means that it can be possible to buy back your 5 option contracts for a small loss and sell the 5 contracts you purchased for a profit at the same time to offset the loss of the contracts you sold.

Another alternative would be to buy back the 5 contracts that you initially sold and continue holding the 5 contracts that you purchased for a bigger profit as the stock price increases. This scenario is allowing you to profit not only on the 500 shares of stock that you own, but also profit on 500 more shares as the option price increases in value.

In a declining Bear market, you might even choose to sell Covered Call Options and buy Put Options at the same time. For instance, you might sell Covered Call Options on your SPY stock, and buy Put Options on the QQQQ (Nasdaq) or the DIA (Dow Jones Industrials). This way you continue to hold your shares generating income on the sale of Covered Calls and if the market is declining, additional money would be made on the Put Options.

Common Sense Conclusion

Options are not lottery tickets. They can be, and some use them as such by buying cheap options for a few pennies that have a strike price (exercise price) considerably higher or lower than the current price of the underlying stock or index fund. These options that are so far out-of-the-money (higher or lower than the current stock price) are only worth anything in the event there is a disaster and the underlying stock price falls dramatically or runs up in value, depending on the type of option purchased.

Buying Put Options is a great strategy to protect your capital during a declining market. Selling Options can also produce steady income while you are simply holding your investments waiting for an advance. Selling Call Options is a bearish approach to the market. Meaning, you are either expecting the stock to continue trading sideways or expecting a decline in the market or your stock, so you sell a call option above the current price. Therefore, as the market declines, your option will not be exercised because the price of the stock has fallen, and whoever purchased the Option would obviously be better off to buy the stock at a lower price in the open market instead of paying more for the stock by exercising the option. Income for you, plain and simple.

Every Investor should be familiar with Options as an added tool to use in either protecting the investments or generating income. As you can see from the previous example, it just makes good Common Sense to use Options. Remember, every individual has only two ways to make money.

With 'Time' or with 'Money'.

There are no other legal ways to make money. So if you have long-term investments that are not producing 'money,' then making those investments work harder for you can benefit you immensely.

"The conventional wisdom has always been, the people who make money in Options, are the SELLERS."

Remember that when you want to generate income from a stock that is not advancing.

CHAPTER EIGHTEEN

Stop Losses

To be a successful investor you must decide on your investing objectives, and then get a strategy that will work for you, and most importantly, establish rules for limiting your losses that you will adhere to. Don't leave it to chance or you'll be left with chump change.

I can't stress enough the importance of a Stop Loss.

It is very simple. When you purchase, know exactly what you're your maximum potential loss will be. Otherwise, you will be just like our buddy that is still holding his 1032 shares of SPY ten years later hoping to break even, someday, maybe.

Let's look at an example of a good Stop Loss. We'll use the SPY 2008-09 chart where the purchase was made at $94.77 per share.

This is a good example because after the purchase, the price was up and down for a few weeks before advancing.

The key to every trade is to limit your loss to no more than 6 to 8%. In this case the purchase was made at $94.77 and an 8% loss would have been selling at $87.18. Therefore, as soon as you made the purchase, you should have entered a Stop Loss to sell your shares if the price drops to $87. That way the maximum amount you would lose is $7.77 per share. It wouldn't matter then if the SPY crossing over to the positive side of the 200 DMA happened to be a false rally in the market and it turned and fell back to its previous low of $68.00, or even lower. You are protected and will not lose more than your set amount.

Don't be greedy or scared and enter a Stop Loss for only a few cents below your purchase. Every stock must have a little breathing room and you don't want to get sold out senselessly. The 6 to 8% rule has been around for years. There is a reason this amount is used for Stop Losses. Meaning, normally if the price drops more than 6 to 8% then there is a valid reason for that much decline. And chances may be pretty good that it will drop further.

If you are 'stopped out', then that does NOT mean you are a bad investor or trader. Remember, no emotion. It would only mean that the purchase was simply made at the wrong time. Losing 6 or 8% is much better than our buddy who is still down 30% or more.

Another very useful technique is to make your purchases in increments. For instance, instead of purchasing all your shares at once, make a purchase of about 25% and watch the price for a few days (with a Stop Loss) until there is an advance and then buy some more in increments. This way if your first purchase is at the wrong time and you are stopped out, then you only lost $7.77 per share on a small number of shares.

Of course as the price increases, then you are profitable and can add to your investment, move your stop loss higher, and even by purchasing more you won't lose any of your capital.

Trailing Stop Loss

Remember when you sold out the last time at $109.11?

The chart we used earlier is shown below again. Notice that SPY reached a price above $120.00 per share before dropping to your sell point of $109.11.

Using a ***Trailing Stop Loss*** can capture more profit for you when used properly. Moving your Stop Loss higher as the stock advances preserves more of your gains. Yes, you will occasionally be sold out and then have to wait for another entry point. But in the event there had been a Trailing Stop Loss in place as SPY was advancing, then instead of selling out at the 200 DMA as you did, you would have been sold out at a higher price.

For instance, if you felt there was a correction in the market due to happen in the near future and placed your Stop Loss at $116 or $118, then you would have benefited by gaining roughly $18,000 by being sold out quicker.

As you can also see, there are many zigs and zags in the price as it advanced during 2009 and 2010. Yes, a stock can trade significantly above the 200 DMA for extended periods of time, but will eventually return to the moving average. In this case, a Trailing Stop Loss would have worked well keeping it low enough to allow 'breathing room' yet higher than the 200 DMA to preserve as much gain as possible.

Creative Stop Losses

Don't Do it! Many brokerage houses allow Stop Losses to be used creatively. Meaning, they allow you to enter different types of Stop Losses, such as a 'Stop Limit' order.

These different types of Stop Losses should be used by ONLY the traders with the ability to watch the market constantly.

To understand how these work, you first have to understand what a Limit Order is, because a Stop Limit Order combines the features of Stop Loss with those of a Limit Order.

A stop-limit order is practical for the individual investor to use when buying, but not when selling. When you are buying, the order will be executed at a specified price (or better) after a given stop price has been reached. Once the stop price is reached, the stop-limit order becomes a limit order to buy (or sell) at the limit price, which is the price you designated, or better.
For example, let's assume that ABC Inc. is trading at $40 and an investor wants to buy the stock once it begins to show some serious upward momentum, as in our examples, maybe crosses above the 200 DMA. The investor has put in a stop-limit order to buy with the stop price at $45 and the limit price at $46.

Now, if the price of ABC Inc. moves above the $45 stop price, the order is activated but NOT filled. Once it is activated, it turns into a limit order, and will only be filled if the price of ABC is under $46 (the limit price). If the stock gaps above $46, the order will not be filled. This protects the buyer from purchasing at 'Market Price' in the event the price is much higher than the $46 limit.

The problem with using the 'Limit' feature in a Stop Loss, is that the trade is not guaranteed to be executed if the price is outside the Limit amount.

For example let's turn the previous example into a sell situation. If the investor owns ABC Inc. and it is trading at $46, but fears the price is going to fall and used a Stop Limit, then it could be disastrous. If a Stop was set at $42 per share and the Limit was $41 per share, then if the price fell to $42 the Stop would activate, but then the Limit Order would be to sell at $41 or Better.

The problem is the Limit. If the price gapped down, or fell quickly to $40.75, the order would not be filled even though the Stop had been activated because the price was not above the $41 limit. So the Investor would still be holding the shares until another order could be placed. This can be dangerous in the event a stock or the market is crashing.

A normal Stop Loss order is simple. It is an order that becomes executable once a set price has been reached and is then filled at the current market price. Yes, in crash situations, you might not get a good-fill, but you would be out and not holding on to a losing situation.

Common Sense Conclusion

There are ONLY TWO things to remember about a Stop Loss.

1) **USE IT!** Without a Stop Loss you are simply flirting with disaster, and sooner, rather than later, you will find it. When you enter into an investment, place your Stop Loss immediately. Always.
2) **Don't Get Creative**

A very good habit to start is, if you place your trade online, then never get up from your computer after you enter your trade without placing your Stop Loss. The Stop Loss IS part of the trade. It is that important.

Regardless, whether you are buying or selling short, a Stop Loss will not eliminate the risk. Risk is always there regardless. But Common Sense certainly tells us that a Stop Loss will 'Limit' the risk. That is what is important. Always place the 'Odds' in your favor and protect your capital.

Thoughts and Summary

"There is only one side of the market and it is not the bull side or the bear side, but the right side."
~Jesse Livermore

Jesse Livermore, whose life as a trader is depicted in the Investment classic, '*Reminiscences of a Stock Operator*', is revered as possibly the greatest trader of all time, and the book encapsulates his career in trading during the early 1900s.

Is the market the same today as it was in the early 1900s?
Is the market the same as it was in the 40s, 50s, 60s, or even the 80s**?** No! The market may not even be the same as it was last year. Nothing stays the same, everything changes.

Realistically, the market during the early 1900s was possibly closer in comparison to the penny stock trading of the 21st century. There are many stories regarding stock market manipulation in the early years, and this was possibly due to the smaller number of shares issued by each company and traded on the exchange at the time. This same type of manipulation with penny stocks happens constantly today on the Internet and in stock market forums with pump and dump scams.

What will be the next Microsoft, Wal-Mart, Google, or Apple? No one knows.
What will take the market to the next new high? Again, no one knows. In the early 1900s it was railroads, autos, and steel. Later it became radio and television. Then it was computers and the Internet. The point is, we live in an ever-changing world which also creates an ever-changing market. Holding investments for long periods of time is a very risky

endeavor. The same companies that propelled the market to new highs in the 1920s, 40s, or 80s, are not the companies that will continue to progress. Even many of the companies of the 90s are no longer a driving force or a good investment. Some are already bankrupt. Times change, people change, companies change, and the market is ever-changing. When trading in the market was opened to the public allowing individuals online access with instantaneous trades, this drastically changed the market. No, this was not a bad thing. But the market can no longer be compared with the way it was at any time throughout history.

The only thing that will continue to be the same relating to the market is fear and greed and the psychology of the traders and investors. That is basic human instinct and is not likely to ever change.

Is there one investment theory or strategy that will work consistently? No!

As you have seen, the buy and hold strategy only works at certain times with certain stocks, and you don't want to be holding on during Secular Bear markets that can last 15 to 20 years. Other strategies will work at certain times and will not work at other times.

That is the reason I have presented you with money making strategies to not only help you stay out of the market during bad times, but also strategies to help you make money on your holdings during times when the market is dead and not advancing. You must decide what will work at any given time.

Numerous stock market "experts" constantly fill the airwaves, magazines, and newsletters offering advice, tips, gimmicks, promises, and scams. When you stand back and look at it logically, it certainly becomes humorous at times. You'll see computer software that will supposedly make money for you while you sleep, hear sales pitches that will 'almost' guarantee you ways to make a profit, and a plethora of Talking Heads of every variety prognosticating what they believe will happen in the future. They all have their very own crystal ball. They are all 'Prophets'. And many of these so-called professionals will make numerous predictions because the law of averages says that eventually they will be right, *ONCE*. Of course when they are correct, that is all you will hear. You will not hear about the 10, 20, or 30 times they were incorrect.

But in reality, the Snake Oil Salesmen have been around for centuries, selling elixirs and potions of all kinds, the only difference is, they have now gone high tech with trading programs, Advisors, get rich quick schemes, and promising profits that never happen.

The problem most people have with the Stock Market is listening to all the sensationalism and hype. The action of the 'Market' does the talking. Pretty much everything else is just 'noise'. It's exactly the same as when you want to know what someone might be up to but you are afraid they aren't telling you the 'whole story'. You don't listen to their words, you watch their actions.

Always use what you have learned and your Common Sense. In a Bull Market, they are all geniuses.

But never forget about the consequences of the inevitable and reoccurring bear markets. This book has provided you with the facts, the history, the tools to always protect your investment capital, and the knowledge to do it yourself.

Never rely on gurus, brokers, or financial advisors to maximize your returns. They have already set the stage to take your money and are just waiting for you to come along. And I can promise you, they won't be there to tell you when it's time to get out. They risk hurting themselves financially if they tell you to sell.

You see, most TV personalities, commentators, and employees of financial news networks are required by their employment contract to place their investments in a Fund. This is an attempt to avoid conflict of interest issues. But think about it. If their money is in a fund that will surely decrease in value with a market decline, the conflict of interest is still present since being Bearish on the market or the economy might entice investors to sell. Any selling will cause a decline, and any decline will result in a decline of their own accounts.

Use what you have learned and select and develop an Investing Plan that is mechanical, non-emotional, an investing approach that you can master so you can make your own independent selection of investments and your own buying and selling decisions. You should feel comfortable with the strategy you select. Make sure you use it with the proper risk-control measures, which means cutting losses quickly. Always place the 'Odds' in your favor.

No one but you has your best interests at heart. You didn't depend on someone else to tell you how to earn your money, and you should never depend on some disinterested so-called "expert" to tell you how to manage it and help it grow. Remember that the overwhelming majority of financial advisors pay absolutely *NO* attention to the market's health and they hardly ever tell you when to sell and will simply never ever tell you to go into cash. They don't believe in technical analysis. They will always focus on selling you on the "story" and the fundamentals, the forecasted earnings, and revenues. That doesn't work, and can frequently backfire on you. Remember, it doesn't matter if a company is having a 'banner year' and producing a 'bumper crop', when the Market heads into a downtrend, the price of all stocks go down and take with them the value out of your investment portfolio.

The strategies I have presented all have as the centerpiece of their performance, the concept of being out of the market when the market is falling or expected to fall. The main concern is to protect your capital and to cut your losses to a maximum of 6 to 8% below your purchase price. Remember the sage advice of financier Bernard Baruch, who said:

> **"Even being right three or four times out of 10 should yield a person a fortune if they have the sense to cut losses quickly."**
> ~ Bernard Baruch

Investors will always be moved by fear and greed. When the market is rising, they look for more and more profits. When the market is falling they become so fearful that they freeze and do nothing. They rationalize it by saying that it is only a "paper" loss, and that history shows that the market "always comes back." They stay the course when they should have acted and acted fast. They put their heads in the sand and pretend that the mounting losses are not happening to them. They think this will blow over and that everything will be fine.

But the losses are real, not paper. As we saw with our Buddy that held his 1032 shares of SPY, ten years and counting, and he was still down nearly 30%. Common Sense Investing attempts to avoid all that. Be true to your investing principles and be true to yourself and using Common Sense in making your Investments can work for you.

Put the odds in your favor and you can avoid the brunt of future bear markets and market corrections. Additionally, you can retain your profits during bull markets while reducing your risk. These benefits are hard to beat.

I hope that this book will help you to think and invest for yourself. May your time be well spent, and may you enjoy many successes in the future. The next step is yours!

Happy Trading,
Fred McAllen
fredmcallen.com

Printed in Poland
by Amazon Fulfillment
Poland Sp. z o.o., Wrocław

21776687R00119